Robin

ELIZABETH OUR QUEEN

RICHARD DIMBLEBY

* * *

ELIZABETH OUR QUEEN

* * *

London
HODDER AND STOUGHTON

FIRST PUBLISHED APRIL 1953

SECOND IMPRESSION APRIL 1953

MADE AND PRINTED IN GREAT BRITAIN FOR
HODDER AND STOUGHTON LTD., LONDON, BY
HAZELL, WATSON AND VINEY, LTD., AYLESBURY AND LONDON

CONTENTS

5

CONTENTS

ILLUSTRATIONS

THE COLOUR PORTRAITS

THE ILLUSTRATIONS IN PHOTOGRAVURE

ILLUSTRATIONS

ILLUSTRATIONS

INTRODUCTION

MANY books have been written that tell the life-story of Her Majesty the Queen; many others, no doubt, are being prepared. They trace, with pictures and a wealth of anecdote, her life from earliest childhood to the present day. Because there is a limit to the number of true stories of Her Majesty's youth and upbringing which are known to writers, there is a similarity among many of these biographies; the same revealing, often amusing, tales appear in slightly differing form. An accurate life-story, after all, can be told only once; thenceforth all other accounts are but variations of the original.

Therefore I have not presumed to write a biography, or "intimate" story, of Her Majesty. Instead, I have tried to tell her story against its splendid background, relating it always to the significance of the monarchy. This is, if you like, a book about the Sovereign, rather than a book about Queen Elizabeth. It gives some account of the Protestant Succession which put the second Elizabeth on the throne. It describes the careful, arduous training that a future queen must undergo, and it attempts, under the title of the "Mantle of Monarchy," to show the significance of the Sovereign in the life of Britain and the Commonwealth today.

Though the reader will find no gossip and little anecdote in this book, I would not like him or her to read it without having clearly in mind a picture of the woman herself who now bears the heavy burden of queenship and who faces the historic ordeal of Coronation. To most of us the Queen is a remote person, seen only occasionally in short flashes of pageantry. The clattering of hooves, the sunshine glinting on a State landau, the scarlet-coated postilions, the sudden notes of the National Anthem, and the Queen has come and gone. Those who were lucky saw her smile and wave across the heads of the crowd; those who were not saw her reflection in a mirror held aloft on a stick or hurriedly snatched from a handbag. Some did not see her at all, but felt the surge of excitement and heard the burst of cheers and clapping as she passed.

How different for the Queen, whose whole public life must be lived in front of crowds, troops, dignitaries, and cameras. The spontaneous applause that rises and falls as she passes is an unbroken sound in her ears, for cheering keeps pace with the royal carriage. Wherever she goes, the music of the Anthem is with her; troops are always motionless at attention; people about her always formal and correct. Everything she does is watched, everything she wears is noted, everything she says treasured and remembered.

It is a tremendous strain that the Throne imposes upon one person. Helped as she is by her husband's presence, there is much that the Queen must do alone, and do with grace and charm. Those who have the opportunity of seeing Her Majesty at close quarters, as I have done, know how greatly she exercises those important qualities. They know, too, how suddenly she can switch from one mood to another, not necessarily because an occasion demands it but because she has a great sense of humour that lies just below the surface, waiting to break through solemnity whenever it can. Photographs rarely do her justice; she is smaller, slimmer, and altogether more lively than they make her. She has a flashing smile that can cut right through the barrier of formality, and a clear, incisive voice. She has, also, a sureness and determination, undoubtedly the result of the years of training, which leave no doubt of her intention and ability to uphold the full authority of the Throne.

I remember watching from a few yards away when Her Majesty made her first appearance after her father's death to distribute the Royal Maundy in Westminster Abbey. With great formality and strictly according to tradition, she was conducted along the lines of men and women waiting to receive alms. Everyone in the great nave of the Abbey who was in a position to see the Queen was watching her, a small figure in black, walking between the taller and splendidly robed officers of the Almonry, the Bishop of Lichfield, and the Dean of Westminster. They saw her pass along the line, smiling at each old man and woman as she handed them their purses of silver coins. It was a formal ceremony, one that had changed greatly since its origin nineteen hundred years ago in the Last Supper. Today, in its abbreviated form, it could have been a quick routine occasion. Not so, however, with the Queen. She paused and made a separate ceremony of the handing-over of each bag of alms. At last she came to a group of half-a-dozen men and women who were blind, and who waited nervously, listening to the footsteps of the Queen and the almoners as they approached. They need not have been uneasy, for Her Majesty looked at them swiftly and, without prompting, took hold of the hand of the first woman, spoke to her, and, lifting her hand, laid a purse in it. She clasped the hand for a moment in her own before moving on.

This may seem a small incident to relate, but it is indicative of the quick sympathy and the willingness to depart suddenly from strict formality that the Queen possesses. While intent on maintaining the true and necessary dignity of the Throne, she is quickly responsive to the mood of every occasion.

As you read this account of the history and significance of the Sovereign, therefore, keep in your mind the picture of an intelligent, alert woman who, burdened by the duty of which she has such a deep sense, has kept in her womanhood all the sense of fun and humour that she possessed as a girl.

A new era for Britain opened in February 1952, when the second Elizabeth came to the throne. No more devoted or courageous person than she could carry on the monarchy which is the enduring strength of Britain and the wonder and envy of a large part of the world.

Part I

BIRTHRIGHT

PROLOGUE

FROM Capetown, South Africa, on the evening of April 21st, 1947, the voice of Princess Elizabeth travelled across the world. For the celebration of her twenty-first birthday the Princess was six thousand miles from the country of her birth, but, as she said, she was not six thousand miles from home. As heiress presumptive to the throne that she must so soon ascend, her home, like that of her father, was wherever the peoples of the British Commonwealth and Empire dwelt.

Following historical precedent and constitutional practice, Princess Elizabeth had come of age at eighteen so far as ability to assume the royal functions of a fully empowered monarch was concerned. Her great-great-grandmother had been only twenty-seven days past her eighteenth birthday when she became Queen Victoria. There is no minimum age at which the heir or heiress succeeds to the throne—Edward IV was only nine at the time of his accession—but if he or she is under the age of eighteen the royal duties are carried out by a regent.

Previously provision for regency had been made specifically on each particular occasion that the necessity arose. George IV, for instance, was appointed Prince Regent during the insanity of his father, George III. At the time of George V's accession, provision was made for Queen Mary to become Regent in the event of the King's incapacity; when King George VI came to the throne, however, it was not the Queen but his brother the Duke of Gloucester who was nominated for the role. Not until

1937 did the Regency Act establish permanent machinery for automatic operation should the sovereign be wholly incapacitated by reason of infirmity of mind or body, or succeed to the throne under the age of eighteen. In either of these events all royal functions would be discharged by the "person next in line of succession to the Crown and not disqualified" as regent. To be regent, however, the person must be over the full age of twenty-one and not eighteen as in the case of a sovereign.

Up to 1943 the curious position existed that although considered capable of reigning at eighteen the heir to the Throne must be twenty-one before acting as Counsellor of State. Consisting of the wife or husband of the sovereign and the four persons next in succession and not disqualified by age or incapacity, the Council of State is appointed to deal with current business requiring the sovereign's approval in time of illness or absence abroad. The Council's powers, however, are strictly limited. The counsellors may not, for example, grant any rank or title and they cannot dissolve parliament unless on the express instructions of the sovereign.

A Regency Bill amendment introduced in 1943 at the personal wish of King George VI made Princess Elizabeth eligible to serve on a Council of State from her eighteenth birthday, and during her father's wartime visits to North Africa and Italy she did in fact act as a counsellor and gained early experience of some of the duties of a sovereign.

The main change wrought in her position by her full legal coming-of-age was that in the event of her father's total incapacity she would become Regent. But Princess Elizabeth's twenty-first birthday marked more than a constitutional change in status. By her own volition it marked with her broadcast her entry into the lives of the peoples of the British Commonwealth and Empire, whatever their race, whatever their tongue: peoples who within five years were to become her subjects.

In 1940 she had broadcast to the children of the Empire. As a child she had spoken as the children's representative and leader, looking already to the time when the perils of war and bitterness of family separation should be ended.

"When peace comes," said the young Princess Elizabeth, "remember it will be for us, the children of today, to make the world of tomorrow a better and happier place."

For those same children, now young men and women, now the youth of the British family of nations, Princess Elizabeth spoke again as representative on her twenty-first birthday.

"Now that we are coming to manhood and womanhood," she said, "it is surely a great joy to us all to think that we shall be able to take some of the burden off the shoulders of our elders who have fought and worked and suffered to protect our childhood. We must not be daunted by the anxieties and hardships that the war has left behind for every nation of our Commonwealth. We know that these things are the price we cheerfully undertook to pay for the high honour of standing alone seven years ago in defence of the liberty of the world. Let us say with Rupert Brooke: 'Now, God be thanked Who has matched us with His hour.'

"I am sure you will see our difficulties in the light that I see them, as the great opportunity for you and me. Most of you have read in the history books the proud saying of William Pitt that England had saved herself by her exertions and would save Europe by her example. But in our time we may say that the British Empire has saved the world first, and has now to save itself after the battle is won. I think that is an even finer thing than was done in the days of Pitt, and it is for us who have grown up in these years of danger and glory to see that it is accomplished in the long years of peace that we all hope stretch ahead.

"If we all go forward together with an unwavering faith, a high courage, and a quiet heart, we shall be able to make of this ancient Commonwealth which we all love so dearly an even grander thing—more free, more prosperous, more happy, and a more powerful influence for good in the world—than it has been in the greatest days of our forefathers. To accomplish that we must give nothing less than the whole of ourselves.

"There is a motto which has been borne by many of my ancestors—a noble motto: 'I Serve.' These words were an inspiration to many bygone heirs to the throne when they made their knightly dedication as they came to manhood. I cannot do quite as they did, but through the invention of science I can do what was not possible for any of them. I can make my solemn act of dedication with a whole Empire listening. I should like to make that dedication now. It is very simple:

"I declare before you all that my whole life, whether it be long or short, shall be devoted to your service and the service of our great imperial family to which we all belong, but I shall not have the strength to carry out this resolution unless you join in it with me, as I now invite you to do.

"I know that your support will be unfailingly given. God help me to make good my vow, and God bless all of you who are willing to share it."

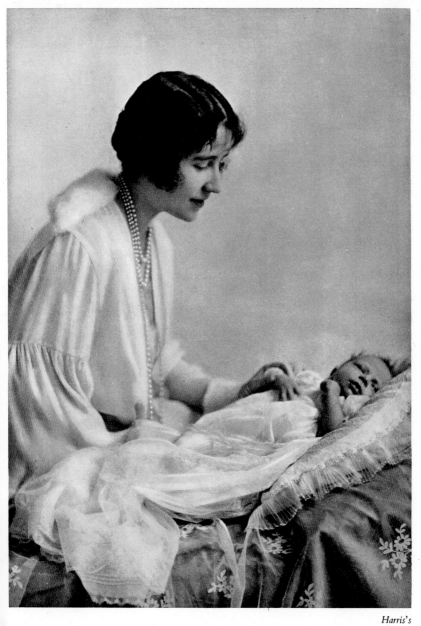

Harris's

Elizabeth our Queen as a baby with her mother, 1926

At Glamis Castle in 1929

2

THE LEGACY OF QUEEN ANNE

WHEN the English monarchy was restored in 1660, Charles II came to a throne stripped of many of its powers. Parliament had summoned the monarch, instead of the monarch summoning parliament, and therein lay the key to the situation. Belief in the Divine Right of Kings was dying, if not dead. In the matters of law and finance the king could act only through parliament. The courts of the royal prerogative were abolished. The king himself could no longer directly impose taxation or proceed against a subject.

Though a Roman Catholic at heart, Charles II agreed politically to uphold the national Church of England. He instructed his brother and heir presumptive, the Duke of York, that his daughters, Mary and Anne, should be brought up in the Protestant faith. The Protestant Succession had not yet, however, been established. The Test Act of 1673, to which Charles was forced to agree, excluded Roman Catholics from office under the Crown, but did not exclude them from the throne itself.

James, the Duke of York, was an avowed Papist. He had been forced to agree to the religious upbringing of Mary and Anne, but when he succeeded his brother as James II there was no question that any issue of the marriage with his second wife, Mary of Modena, would be brought up in anything but the Roman Catholic faith. If, therefore, a son were born, Mary and Anne, on whom the Protestants pinned their hopes, would be excluded in favour of a Roman Catholic heir.

With so much dependent upon the outcome, constant rumours about the Queen's condition inevitably arose: rumours encouraging the hopes of the Papists and inciting the suspicions of the Protestants.

Anne wrote to her sister Mary, who had married William III of Orange: "That they [the Papists] will stick at nothing, be it never so wicked, if it will promote their interests, gives some cause to fear there may be foul play."

Anne was at Bath when the news came that the Queen had given birth to a son, James Edward, on June 10th, 1688. The fact that Anne was away from her stepmother, that the Archbishop of Canterbury was absent, and that those at Court at the time were mainly Papists gave spur to Protestant rumours and disclaimers. According to gossip at Court, they maintained, the Queen had had a miscarriage at Easter. The child now claimed as heir apparent could not therefore be the Queen's, but must have been smuggled into her apartments in a warming-pan.

Anne herself was unable to make up her mind about the truth. "It may be it is our brother," she wrote to Mary, "but God only knows, for she never took care to satisfy the world or give people any demonstration of it."

Today historians generally agree that James Edward, the "Old Pretender," was in fact the lawful son of James II and rightful heir to the Throne. In any case, it was probably not so much doubt about the birth as the alternatives facing the country that caused parliament ultimately to invite Mary and her husband, William of Orange, to take over the throne from James II as joint sovereigns.

On the Continent the persecution of the Protestants, particularly in France, served as a warning of what might recur here if James succeeded in his attempts to re-establish "Popery." Already the country had recoiled from the savage travesty of justice meted out by Judge Jeffreys. The accession of James Edward would mean a continuation and strengthening of his father's efforts and probably lead to a line of kings with powerful Papist convictions and a dominating foreign influence. James Edward was the son of an Italian princess, whereas his half-sisters, Mary and Anne, were daughters of an English lady, Anne Hyde. When Anne followed Mary and William to the throne, the point she proudly made in her accession speech to parliament was the fact that her heart was "entirely English."

The death of Anne's son, William of Gloucester, at the age of eleven, ended hopes of a direct Protestant succession from the House of Stuart. Provision was therefore made by the Act of Settlement in 1701 that in the event of Anne's death without issue the Crown should pass to the Electress Sophia of Hanover, granddaughter of James I, and her heirs, provided they were Protestant. The Act further stipulated that no sovereign who became a Papist or married a Papist could occupy the throne. Thus was established the Protestant Succession that has now brought the Crown to our Queen Elizabeth.

One other twentieth-century outcome of the rumours and suspicions attending the birth of James Edward was the summoning of the Home Secretary, Sir William Joynson-Hicks, to the Earl of Strathmore's London house, No. 17 Bruton Street, on the night of April 20th/21st, 1926. There, on behalf of parliament and the people, to witness that there was no substitution or subterfuge, the Home Secretary was shown the royal baby soon after the birth at 2.40 a.m.

Subsequently Sir William Joynson-Hicks recorded that the infant, first daughter of the Duke and Duchess of York and fourth lady in the land, had yawned at him. Perhaps she was already expressing an opinion of a formality long outmoded, for Queen Elizabeth will be the last sovereign to whom it has applied. When Prince Charles, the heir apparent, was born, the Home Secretary, at the express wish of King George VI, did not attend, and the custom bequeathed from the days of James II and "the warming-pan plot" came to an end.

3

LOYALTIES

CHRISTENED Elizabeth Alexandra Mary after her mother, great-grandmother, and grandmother respectively, Princess Elizabeth was the first royal infant to be baptised in the private chapel of Buckingham Palace.

There was no sign then to indicate the destiny that awaited her. On the throne her grandfather, King George V, was consolidating the position of the Crown as the head of a family at a time when monarchy throughout Europe was at a discount. Though Britain herself was seething with internal unrest that during the first month of Princess Elizabeth's life was to flare into the General Strike, it was directed at neither king nor kingship. Rather, the Crown was gaining new power out of internal discord. Just as it served as the link with Empire, so now the Crown became the symbol of unity holding together a nation divided by political and industrial strife. The value of a monarch above politics, to watch like a kindly, impartial father over the conflicting elements of his family and to see that the true will of the electorate prevailed, was becoming more and more widely recognised.

In the Prince of Wales, then thirty-two years old and the most eligible bachelor in the world, was one of the most popular heirs to the throne of all time. Setting a new conception of royalty in the freedom and informality with which he travelled the world and mixed with the people at large, his succession as "the people's king" was already being heralded with high hopes.

The mantle of monarchy seemed far removed from both the baby princess and her father, the Duke of York, who had been brought up as a younger son to support his brother and remain in the background. With that position the Duke was undoubtedly content. A natural reserve and slight stammer were no great impediment in a supporting role which, although it called for a share of royal duties, allowed him his vocation of the sea, his own choice of public service in boys' clubs, and the summer camp where he brought rich and poor together in one brotherhood, and the life of a country squire between times.

It was as the daughter of a country gentleman, therefore, that Princess Elizabeth's upbringing began. True, as the first royal grandchild and with no family of the Prince of Wales to divert the spotlight, the young princess was photographed and subjected to a glare of publicity and adulation such as no child before had ever received; but if, away from her parents, there was ever any sign of crowd worship turning the head of a child, there was always Queen Mary ready to take restraining measures.

Like most children, Princess Elizabeth shared her childhood visits between her respective grandparents. In her mother's home at Glamis, where her sister Princess Margaret was born, the future queen played against the romantic background of Scottish history. Here, in the oldest family residence in Britain, King Malcolm was murdered in 1033. This was the castle so greatly coveted by James V that he had the rightful owner, widow of the sixth Lord Glamis, burned at the stake on a fabricated charge of witchcraft, and took possession before her ashes were cool. Here the Old Pretender held court; and here, too, lay the famous room of mystery, of which the location and secret that it contains are reputed to be known only to three persons at any one time—the master, the heir, and the steward of Glamis.

Let Queen Anne boast that she was "entirely English"; Queen Elizabeth can claim with truth that she is indeed British. England and Scotland are united in the Crown not only politically but by birth.

The first awareness of monarchy must have been puzzling to the childhood princess. Here was the King, treated by all with homage and respect, though the child knew he was really a benevolent grandfather ready to play and to pamper her, and not in the least frightening or awe-inspiring. The love between them was deep and real, and it was the three-years-old Princess who, with her first opportunity of national service, was sent with medical approval to cheer and inspire King George V's recovery from his long illness of 1928-9. One hour with his granddaughter, King George is reported to have declared subsequently, did him more good than all the medicine the royal physicians could prescribe. When, restored to reign for another seven years, he returned from Bognor and appeared on the balcony at Buckingham Palace to acknowledge the sympathy and rejoicing of his people, Princess Elizabeth was at his side making her first public appearance, waving and blowing kisses to the crowd.

Outside her parents, however, it was the influence of her grandmother, Queen Mary, that was to play the greatest part in shaping the character of the future Queen Regnant. Queen Victoria herself had made up her mind that her god-daughter, the Princess May of Teck, was one day to be queen. When she did come to the Throne as the Queen Consort of George V, Queen Mary was moulded in her godmother's views on both the Crown and the place of woman in public life. Nothing must be done to divert the spotlight from the sovereign. Whatever her station, a woman's place was in the background supporting her husband, not drawing attention to herself by indulgence in public speech-making. On the latter point, changing times may have modified Queen Mary's outlook so far as others are concerned, though she herself has departed from neither. Queen Mary established a pattern both for regal queenliness and dignified womanhood and lived to it, and into that pattern in 1923 she smoothly guided the Lady Elizabeth Bowes-Lyon who, not being of the Blood Royal, might well have been overwhelmed by the new life thrust upon her with her elevation to Duchess of York and wife of the King's second son.

As queen consort, queen mother, and now queen grandmother, Queen Mary has always been most particular about emphasising the precedence of the Crown, no matter whose the head upon which it rests. The Duke of Windsor has related how, on his first meeting with his mother after his accession as Edward VIII, Queen Mary at once came forward and kissed his hand. When Queen Elizabeth returned on that tragic flight from Nairobi a letter from Queen Mary awaited her at the airport; it was signed "Your loving grandmother and subject."

In public life, whatever had to be done Queen Mary did swiftly and to the point. Whatever had to be declared open or named, she declared open or named in a sentence. There was never an accompanying speech. Her sole broadcast consists of twenty-eight words with which she christened the liner that bears her name. On one occasion, however, in a brief talk to a party of children from Dr. Barnardo's Homes who were emigrating to Australia, she gave them a code for living; a code

In London at the time of the late Duke of Kent's wedding, 1934

Leaving a bookshop with her sister in 1935

that was her own way of life and a code that sums up her influence upon her granddaughter.

"Remember," Queen Mary said, "that life is made up of loyalty: loyalty to your friends; loyalty to things beautiful and good; loyalty to the country in which you live; loyalty to your king; and, above all, for this holds all other loyalties together, loyalty to God."

4

TWO FATEFUL YEARS

ROYALTY in rejoicing, royalty in death, royalty in crisis: within two years the meaning of the Throne was thrust vividly upon a young princess in a manner that could not have been more dramatic.

Princess Elizabeth was nine years old on that day in May 1935 when, to the sound of bugles and the clattering hooves of the escort of Household Cavalry, the carriage in which she rode with her parents and sister wheeled out of the courtyard at Buckingham Palace to join the pageantry of the procession to St. Paul's Cathedral to celebrate in thanksgiving the Silver Jubilee of the reign of King George V. The day was as bright and fair as any in the traditional month of merry-making. The nation was *en fête*, and the people seized gladly the opportunity of a brief escape from the tension of the storm clouds that were gathering over Europe.

On the Continent ancient monarchies had been swept away and substituted with dictatorships based on government by armed thugs, concentration camps, and a brutality that exceeded the tortures of the Dark Ages. A power-mad Hitler had contemptuously torn up the Treaty of Versailles and was openly rearming Germany. The ineffectualness of the League of Nations, on which so many had pinned their hopes for peace, had been shown up by the defiance and departures from membership of first Japan and then Hitler. Already Mussolini was preparing to deal the League a death-blow by Italy's invasion of Abyssinia.

Britain turned with relief to rejoice in a celebration which was more than that of the personal jubilee of King George V. It was an occasion to do honour to him as a man who had grown to be trusted and respected and who, in the words of the Archbishop of Canterbury of the time, had fulfilled the "ideal of sovereignty based on service"; but it was also the opportunity to give thanks for the heritage of a unique and stable form of government that had been developed through the centuries. George V was, in person, the symbol of the country, and in rejoicing for him the nation rejoiced also for itself.

For King George V, alas, the Silver Jubilee was the Indian Summer. Just over eight months later his life "passed peacefully to its close" and Princess Elizabeth, with Queen Mary, her mother, Queen Maud of Norway, and the Princess Royal rode in the solitary carriage drawn by a pair of Windsor Greys in the slow, solemn procession that bore George V to his last resting-place. In front walked the foreign monarchs and potentates; her father and uncles Henry of Gloucester and George of Kent. There was the lone figure of the new king, Edward the Eighth, following immediately behind the gun-carriage on which the draped coffin was drawn by a detachment of naval ratings.

As in many a family the first experience of death had come to a child through the loss of a beloved grandparent; but whereas the average child of nine or ten is sheltered as much as possible from the rigours of bereavement, the young princess by reason of her birth had to meet death in all its fullness and solemn majesty. With a dignity and composure, already noticeably regal, she endured the ordeal of the funeral.

Noise and excitement, cheering crowds and waving flags,

had greeted the Silver Jubilee drive. Now all was hushed: the slow march, the muffled drums, the haunting Funeral March, the lament of the pipes. The crowds were there, but they were still and silent, heads uncovered and bowed. They had come not to enjoy the spectacle of pageantry but to render homage, to pay a personal tribute and demonstrate sympathetically a love and loyalty which because of its muteness was more affecting than the wildest cheers. Thus Princess Elizabeth saw the affection that her grandfather had earned from his subjects; and thus a practical understanding of the symbolism and perpetuity of the Throne must have come to her. For this was a tribute to George V, the man: the King did not die.

"The King is dead. Long live the King!" For over a thousand years of monarchy since Egbert began to reign in A.D. 827 as the first King of the English, the cry has been heard. Only once, during the eleven years of the Cromwellian Protectorate, has the continuity of the Crown been seriously interrupted. But there was a day too, more recently, when the country was without a sovereign: December 11th, 1936.

To ten-years-old Princess Elizabeth the abdication of the immensely popular King Edward VIII, her own childhood hero, "Uncle David," must have been the cruellest lesson in the burdens and responsibilities of constitutional monarchy.

Although members of the royal family need to obtain the consent of the sovereign, declared under the Great Seal, before they can marry, the sovereign himself requires no consent to make his marriage legal. Whomsoever he marries, however, automatically becomes queen, and any children of the marriage are in direct line of succession to the Throne. The people therefore are directly interested in the choice of the sovereign's consort. There is no such thing in British law as a

Dorothy Wilding

The Coronation group, 1937

On board the Royal Yacht in August 1938

morganatic marriage in which the wife of the sovereign retains her own status, and both she and her children are excluded from the throne. To make such a situation possible would require the passing of special legislation to meet the particular instance that arose. In the case of the 1936 constitutional crisis parliament was not prepared to introduce legislation of this nature, and by reason of divorce the lady whom the King wished to marry was not acceptable as Queen to a large section of the community.

Finding it "impossible to carry the heavy burden of responsibility and discharge his duties as King as he would wish to do without the help and support of the woman he loved," King Edward VIII chose to abdicate rather than split the nation and Empire with dissension.

Throughout the days of crisis the nation looked to Queen Mary, whose character, inspiration, and example held firm a monarchy that might have been irreparably damaged. In that time of personal sorrow over her uncle, Princess Elizabeth must have grown aware of the increasing stature of her grandmother and her influence for all that was good and proper in constitutional monarchy. When private grief and bewilderment were forgotten there remained for all time the lessons that emerged, confirmed and strengthened, from the trial.

A king cannot live for himself. In the lines from Shakespeare's *Hamlet* which Mr. Stanley Baldwin, the Prime Minister, quoted in the House of Commons at the time:

> "His will is not his own . . .
> He may not, as unvalued persons do,
> Carve for himself; for on his choice depends
> The safety and the health of this whole state."

Only upon the solid foundation of integrity could the Crown inspire the confidence that was a safeguard against the evils of naziism, fascism, and communism that were afflicting other countries. In that integrity lie the value and power of the traditions that are our heritage and source of greatness.

The Instrument of Abdication which King Edward VIII signed on December 10th, 1936, was without precedent. By it the succession under the Act of Settlement was broken, and the passing of the Crown to the next heir under the Act could not therefore be regarded as automatic. The successor to King Edward VIII must be named, and naturally he must be willing to accept the Crown. There were rumours, in fact, that the Duke of York, who was no longer obliged to follow automatically to the Throne as he would have been in the event of Edward VIII's death, might refuse the offer. His desire, evinced by actual practice, to bring up his daughters in as simple and normal a life as possible was well known. When the call came, however, the Duke, disregarding any personal considerations or wishes, freely accepted the onerous demand of duty both for himself and his heirs.

On December 12th, 1936, at the Palace of St. James, Sir Gerald Wollaston, Garter King-of-Arms, proclaimed with all traditional pomp and ceremony:

"Whereas by an instrument of abdication dated the tenth day of December, his former Majesty King Edward VIII did declare his irrevocable determination to renounce the Throne for himself and his descendants, and the said instrument of abdication has now taken effect whereby the Imperial Crown of Great Britain, Ireland, and all other of his former Majesty's Dominions is now solely and rightfully come to

34

the high and mighty Prince Albert Frederick Arthur George…"

The throne had passed to one who, as his brother said in his farewell broadcast, had "one matchless blessing, enjoyed by so many of you and not bestowed on me, a happy home with his wife and children." Of the strength derived from that "matchless blessing" King George VI was always the first to admit. During the next fifteen years the constant phrase "the Queen and I" in broadcasts and speeches was to become a signature theme beloved of his peoples.

Meanwhile, at the age of ten years and eight months, Princess Elizabeth had become heiress presumptive to the throne.

5

"KING OF THIS REALM"

FOR the first time in history both the queen mother and the heiress to the throne were present at the crowning of a Sovereign. There had been doubt whether Queen Mary would attend her son's coronation—it was not the usual custom for the queen mother to be present—but knowing the deep affection and veneration in which she was held, King George VI decided not only upon her attendance but that she should have her own procession into Westminster Abbey.

Separated from their parents and in the care of their aunt, the Princess Royal, Princess Elizabeth and her sister had driven in their own coach to Westminster and led the procession of the Princes and Princesses of the Blood Royal into the Abbey. They had watched the majestic entry of Queen Mary and her retinue, and had followed their grandmother into the royal box at the side of the High Altar. Perhaps already conscious of her newly-elevated position and the dignity it demanded, the eleven-years-old heiress presumptive tried hard not to be drawn into the exuberant whisperings of her younger sister, who in her excitement nearly lost her robe of purple velvet.

The trumpets sounded a fanfare, and into a scene already resplendent with colour and magnificence came the even greater spectacle of the royal procession—the high dignitaries of the Church and their gleaming crosses, the proud standards of the United Kingdom and the Empire, the Royal Standard, and then the Queen, greeted by shouts of "Vivat Regina Elizabetha." Following came the King's Regalia: high-ranking officers of the three Services bearing the Sword of the Defender of the Faith, the sharp-pointed Sword of Justice, and the blunted Sword of Mercy. Then, with his retinue of bishops and attendants and train-bearers, Princess Elizabeth saw her father himself in the long, ermine-edged, crimson robe of State. From the King's Scholars of Westminster School soared the triumphant acclaim: "Vivat, vivat, Rex Georgius."

When, sixteen years later, the royal procession next entered the Abbey, the Princess herself would be the principal in the centuries-old ceremonial, and the Westminster schoolboys traditionally acclaiming her on behalf of the people, would once again be Queen's Scholars, the forty Queen's Scholars for whom the first Queen Elizabeth founded the school, saying in her Charter of Incorporation: "The Lord pour forth His spirit upon you, that this our College from age to age may bring forth fruits of holiness and learning, ripe and abundant."

In the days of the Witan, the Great Council of the Anglo-Saxons, the king owed his throne to election; and so today in the twentieth century the sovereign is still presented to the people that they may show their recognition and "good liking." Thus in his turn King George VI faced first east, then south, west, and north, whilst four times the Archbishop of Canterbury proclaimed in a loud voice:

"Sirs, I here present unto you, King George, your undoubted King. Wherefore all you who are come this day to do your homage and service, are you willing to do the same?"

Each time back echoed the loud and joyful acclamation: "God Save the King!" The people had shown their willingness and wished the coronation of their new King to proceed.

By the Coronation Oath—the Triple Oath that in essence

remains little changed from the days of the Saxons, and by which the second Queen Elizabeth would also reaffirm her dedication to service—King George VI bound himself by contract with his peoples. Solemnly he swore to govern them in whatever part of the Commonwealth they lived according to their respective laws and customs; to do his utmost to cause law and justice, in mercy, to be executed in all his judgments; and to maintain the laws of God, the true profession of the Gospel, the Protestant Reformed Religion in the United Kingdom, the Settlement of the Church of England, and the rights and privileges of Church and clergy.

It is not only through the laws of the realm which establish him on the throne that the king reigns, but also by the grace of God. The king is both knight and priest. And so after the preparatory Communion Service with the same Gospel reading from St. Matthew that has been heard by our kings and queens for over a thousand years—the verses containing that immortal reply: "Render therefore unto Cæsar the things which are Cæsar's, and unto God the things that are God's"—the Coronation ceremony moved from the earthly to the spiritual. Throughout our history only two kings have refused to take the Sacrament: James II, on religious grounds; and John, of Magna Carta memory, who behaved scandalously, treating the whole of the coronation with unseemly levity and laughter.

Divested of his royal robes and in a simple white shirt and breeches, King George VI, with true humility, took his seat on St. Edward's Chair, hewn out of English oak in the fourteenth century. Above his head a canopy of gold was stretched by four Knights of the Garter. There, Princess Elizabeth saw the mystical anointing of her father, as once Solomon was anointed king by Zadok the priest and Nathan the prophet.

38

On King George VI's hands, his breast, the crown of his head, the Archbishop of Canterbury inscribed the figure of the Cross with consecrated oil from the golden Ampulla, fashioned in the form of an eagle.

The anointing of kings is older than history. Amongst primitive races the rite was considered to endow the recipient with magical powers. In the Christian Church, Thomas Becket interpreted the unction, or anointing, as imparting the seven-fold gifts of the Holy Spirit, or, in particular, glory, fortitude, and knowledge.

Anointed, in the words of the Archbishop, "blessed, and consecrated King over the Peoples whom the Lord your God has given you to rule and govern," George VI became a mortal symbol of an immortal conception. He was the Lord's anointed: in him merged both the secular and the divine ideas of kingship.

To mark his consecrated state the King was first robed with the counterparts of the garments of priesthood before being invested with the insignia of sovereignty. Then his knighthood was recognised. His heels were touched with the Golden Spurs of St. George, emblem of chivalry. By rights he should have been girt with the Sword of State, which signifies justice, the protection of the Church, the defence of widows and orphans, and the punishment and reformation of what is amiss; but the two-handed, double-edged Sword of State is too massive to be girt about any man's waist. In its place, therefore, the Lord Great Chamberlain fixed to the King's golden belt the smaller Sword of Offering.

Rising, the King ungirded the sword and, bearing it flat in his two hands, carried it to the High Altar into the keeping of God. However, as this Sword of Offering was a substitute for the Sword of State and consequently an earthly possession of the King and not a relic of the regalia, it was redeemed upon payment of one hundred shillings by the Marquess of Zetland, who had previously borne the Sword of State. Thereafter the Marquess carried instead the unsheathed Sword of Offering.

The Imperial Robe, a mantle of gold embroidered with roses, was buckled across the King's chest. The richly jewelled Orb surmounted by a cross, symbol of Christ's dominion over the world, was placed in the King's hand by the Archbishop, who then placed on the fourth finger of his right hand the King's Ring, emblem of kingly dignity and the defence of the Christian faith. With that ring the Sovereign becomes virtually wedded to the nation.

Now came the Archbishop with two golden rods, the Sceptre with the Cross, from which shone the "Great Star of Africa" stone cut from the Cullinan diamond; and the Sceptre topped with the image of a dove, symbol of equity and mercy.

"Receive the Royal Sceptre, the ensign of kingly power and justice," said the Archbishop, passing the Sceptre with the Cross into the King's right hand. He then delivered into the King's left hand the Sceptre with the Dove with the injunction: "Be so merciful that you be not too remiss; so execute justice that you forget not mercy. Punish the wicked, protect and cherish the just, and lead your people in the way wherein they should go."

To an eleven-year-old princess, no matter how well she may have been primed by her grandmother or aunt in the ancient rites of the ceremonial, the moment, thrilling above all, that she and her sister must have been awaiting was the self-explanatory climax of the service: the moment when she saw the Archbishop of Canterbury raise aloft the Crown of England. As the Crown was lowered on to her father's head a thousand voices in the Abbey acclaimed him with the cry, "God Save the King!" A cry that at once sped round the world as silver trumpets, rolling drums, saluting guns, and pealing bells heralded the news that a new sovereign had been crowned.

One more presentation to the King remained, the gift of the Bible—"the most valuable thing that this world affords: wisdom, royal law, and the lively oracles of God"—before he was lifted on to the Throne to assume his kingdom. The drums rolled, the trumpets sounded their fanfare, and the Westminster Scholars in their traditional role of the people, led the congregation in the Biblical salutation:

> "God Save King George!
> Long Live King George!
> May the King Live for Ever!"

After the lords spiritual and temporal had paid homage to their new sovereign, the ceremonial anointing and crowning of the Queen Consort followed; and, as the Archbishop placed upon Queen Elizabeth's head the "Crown of glory, honour, and joy" from which sparkled the famous Koh-i-noor diamond, so Princess Elizabeth, Heiress Presumptive, together with the peeresses, put on her coronet—a golden circlet, lightweight when compared with the Crown of England, St. Edward's Crown, that would next be placed upon her head in Westminster Abbey. Distinct from the Imperial State Crown, which is studded with sapphires, rubies, and diamonds, and is worn on State occasions, St. Edward's Crown is used only for the Coronation Service. It is a circlet of gold with four crosses alternating with fleur-de-lys, on a cap of crimson velvet, and surmounted with the Orb and Cross, and weighs five pounds. It is a "Crown of pure gold": a "Crown of glory and righteousness."

Part II

TRAINING FOR THE THRONE

6

CONSTANT PURPOSE

NOT since James II abdicated in 1688 had a sovereign ceased to occupy the throne for any reason but death. Possession of the crown for life was regarded as an integral part of the constitution, a factor as immutable as the laws of nature. Upon King George VI, therefore, lay the immediate and additional responsibility of remedying the shock that had inevitably been caused to the system of constitutional monarchy by the 1936 crisis. Any fears that the new King, who had reached middle age without any specific training for the throne and who had hitherto been outshone by the personal magnetism of his brother, would find the heavy task beyond him were quickly set at naught. He had declared to the Accession Council his "adherence to the strict principles of constitutional government and resolve to work, before all else, for the welfare of the British Commonwealth of Nations." In his message to the Empire at the New Year of 1937 he announced that he had shouldered his responsibilities "with all the more confidence in the knowledge that the Queen and my mother, Queen Mary, are at my side."

The word "monarchy" is derived from two Greek words meaning "rule alone"; from the start, however, King George VI was introducing a new conception and making monarchy a family crown. As the nation depended for stability and greatness upon a strong, moral family life, so too the throne settled down securely as a symbol based upon the firm foundation of family unity and strength. It was "the Queen and I" who pledged themselves to national service and prayed God for guidance and strength to follow the path that lay before them, and when the time came for Princess Elizabeth to begin making speeches the words "my father" instinctively followed any reference to the King.

"The King, my father." Though home was now a palace, much more important was the fact that the palace was a home in the true Christian meaning of the word, although duties of State robbed the King and Queen of many hours that they would have liked to spend with their children. To King George VI and Queen Elizabeth now fell also the question of bringing up not only a daughter but a future sovereign. True, Princess Elizabeth was simply heiress presumptive, but the probability of a male heir to displace her inheritance was becoming remote. As parents, both the King and Queen naturally wished to continue the policy they had established as Duke and Duchess of York, of shielding their daughter from too much limelight. On the other hand, neither wanted to repeat the mistake made in the case of their great-grandmother, who lived so much in the shadows that when she emerged suddenly as Queen Victoria she was both unknown to the people and untrained in public life. So much, in fact, had she been kept under the Duchess of Kent's wing that her first act upon accession was to order the removal of her bed from her mother's room and to have for the first time in her life a room to herself.

A policy of the gradual introduction of Princess Elizabeth to public life was therefore adopted. Naturally, it began with youth movements and interests. She became an enthusiastic Girl Guide in Buckingham Palace's own company; and at twelve took her first presidency—that of the Children's

League of the Princess Elizabeth of York Hospital in the East End of London.

Her education had already been planned on a wider scale than that of the standard school curriculum, with emphasis on those subjects which were of particular importance to the Princess. For that reason, with the agreement of the Sovereign, King George V, and the government, both of whom were constitutionally interested in the education of those in direct succession to the throne, Princess Elizabeth had not gone to any school, but had been taught privately by a Scots governess since she was seven. Prior to that her mother had supervised her initial instruction in reading, writing, and conversational French, as well as deportment, dancing, and the piano.

Now, as heiress presumptive, the scope of her education was broadened still farther. In particular, constitutional history and the evolution of the monarchy became subjects for study in the utmost detail. Important, too, was a sound knowledge of the histories of the Commonwealth. Later it was considered highly desirable that a future sovereign should also be well versed in the affairs of our chief wartime ally and partner in the ideals of the "Four Freedoms" and democratic way of life, and Princess Elizabeth became the first heir to the throne to read American history. The staff of tutors to the Princess grew. In addition to her governess, Miss Marion Crawford, French and German teachers took over the tuition of their national languages, and Canon Crawley of St. George's Chapel, Windsor, was made responsible for both religious instruction and studies in scriptural history.

From the outstanding figures in the world of education Sir Henry Marten, then vice-provost of Eton, was selected as Princess Elizabeth's chief tutor responsible for her advanced and specialised studies, particularly in the various fields of history. "To have a mind capable of mastering things is far more important than the knowledge you actually get," Sir Henry once said, and this was an outlook with which George VI was much in sympathy. He had himself decided that his daughter's lessons in constitutional history should follow the lines of those that he and his brother, the Duke of Windsor, had received from the late Lord Elton, who instead of giving conventional lectures had talked about and discussed the subject with his royal pupils.

Sir Henry Marten gave his first impression of his important charge as "a somewhat shy girl of thirteen who when asked a question would look for confidence and support to her governess—an unnecessary action as I thought, because the answer was almost invariably correct."

Meanwhile, with the King and Queen away on the royal tour of Canada in the spring of 1939, Queen Mary, in whose charge the princesses were left, took a hand in shaping the practical education of the heiress presumptive. It was not enough, Queen Mary considered, for a future queen to read about the treasures and institutions of the national heritage: she must see them for herself. Accordingly, Princess Elizabeth and her sister were taken on a series of informal visits to museums, art galleries, and historic buildings like the Tower of London; from her own wide knowledge and love, Queen Mary inspired in her granddaughter an appreciation of beauty and a feeling for the stirring wealth of history and tradition upon which the Princess in her turn would ultimately make an impression. But life is confined neither to the past nor to beauty and so, as Princess Elizabeth grew older, the scope of her practical education broadened. Princess Elizabeth took in her stride

Baron

H.M. Queen Mary

Bar...
The late King and the Queen Mother, photographed in Buckingham Palac...

commercial institutions, factories, workshops, the Bank of England, and the Royal Mint, seeing how things were done and meeting the people who did them.

From the distinguished strangers' gallery in the House of Commons she listened to the making of the laws of the country, the laws by which her own sovereignty would be established, the laws through which the people themselves consented to be governed, the laws of the constitution that she would solemnly vow to uphold. In the Courts of Justice she saw the same law in operation—"law and justice in mercy being executed in all judgments." Again, these were no visits specially prepared beforehand. Just as the Princess had mingled unnoticed with everyday passengers on Underground and bus, so she arrived unheralded in court on a day when a particularly unsavoury case was being tried. In the view of her parents this was an advantage rather than an embarrassment. Their wish was always for their daughter to gain first-hand knowledge of affairs as they were, not as they appeared through rose-tinted spectacles.

Whatever the situation or crisis that their daughter might meet, they were happy in the knowledge that she would be equipped to face it with the moral strength and character derived from the solid foundation of a good home life and united family, a blessing to which she was to pay repeated tribute later in her public speeches.

"It has become increasingly unfashionable to believe in fixed standards of morality, even if those standards have stood the test of nearly two thousand years," Princess Elizabeth told the people of Wales when she accepted the Freedom of Cardiff in 1948. "We cannot then blame children whose upbringing in some cases hardly gives them a chance to know the difference between right and wrong. It is so often conditions at home which are responsible. I myself have been extremely lucky in this respect and I can speak with feeling of the advantages which a happy family life bring to a child."

Both Queen Victoria and King Edward VII and, to a lesser degree, King George V, had brought up their children on the Victorian theory that strength of character could be fashioned only by severity and repression, and because of their position three generations of royal children had found themselves the luckless examples to which this principle had been applied without any of the compromise or moderation that the average child of their times might have expected.

There was nothing austere or even prim about Princess Elizabeth's upbringing. Her character was developed by "that best of disciplines, founded on respect for what is right, as well as on affection" and an absence of "foolish spoiling." It was an upbringing that brought not priggishness but true joy.

"In the days of my childhood," Princess Elizabeth once remarked, "the sun seemed always to be shining."

7

THE WAR YEARS

"WE shall fight on the beaches, we shall fight on the landing-grounds, we shall fight in the fields and in the streets, we shall fight in the hills; we shall never surrender."

In those grave months of 1940 when France fell and Britain was rallying under the Prime Minister's inspiring exhortation to repel a German invasion that seemed imminent, many who had the means to do so sent their children overseas to Canada and the United States. A large section of public opinion thought that Princess Elizabeth and her sister should join the emigration to safety in Canada.

To pressure from all quarters, however, the King and Queen remained firm. They were not in a position, they considered, to allow themselves the indulgence of their feelings and concern as parents. The departure of the princesses from the country would provide the Germans with a powerful weapon of propaganda and possibly inflict a damaging blow to morale at home at a time when it was vital to stamp out all sense of defeatism. In addition, as the "First Family" they were representative of all Britain's families. Most people had no choice in the matter, but had to "stay put," and in their sense of unity with the rest of the nation the King and Queen decided that they wished to share whatever risks other families might have to run. In this decision they were certainly supported by Mr. Churchill who, when asked to send a message by an emigrating child to the Prime Minister of Canada, informed his Home

Secretary that if he sent any message at all it would be one deprecating any stampede from the country at that time. Only if Hitler made good his vain boast of marching into London would plans already prepared by Cabinet and Service chiefs be put into operation, and the two princesses evacuated with their father and mother to continue the fight from the Dominions. It was therefore at Windsor, under a veil of strict secrecy, that the princesses spent the greater part of the war.

To many the war brought new surroundings, new acquaintances, new comradeships. To Princess Elizabeth it gave an opportunity of meeting and mixing with her future subjects on a scale that might not otherwise have been possible.

With her sister Margaret she joined evacuee children in village concerts in aid of the comforts funds for the forces; and thus, for the first time in the history of entertainment, a "one-night stand" in a village hall received the honour of a royal command repeat performance at Windsor Castle. This encouragement spurred Princess Elizabeth's interest in amateur theatricals to greater efforts, out of which sprang first a nativity play and then the famous Windsor pantomimes that became a feature of the royal family's wartime Christmases. Her repertoire expanded to include singing, dancing, dramatic recitations, and ukulele-playing. As the heiress presumptive to the Throne gave troops stationed in the district a brief respite from the grave task before them by leading them in community singing, Private Atkins must have wondered whether he had not perchance wandered into Ruritania. The Princess became active too in the Sea Rangers Amateur Theatrical Society. The King was invited to one production that she had organised, and Princess Elizabeth must have known all the trepidation suffered by children over parents' appearance and deportment at

school functions, for Princess Margaret was despatched with a message asking the King to be sure to attend in naval uniform as the concert was "a naval occasion."

The war accelerated also Princess Elizabeth's assumption of the leadership of her own generation. Just as the King, more than ever in time of war, was the link between the nations of the British Commonwealth and the symbol of the united struggle, so the Princess became the link between the children of those countries. On October 13th, 1940, the thirteen-and-a-half-year-old Princess emerged publicly as their leader and representative with a broadcast in the Children's Hour to the children of the Empire. Facing the ordeal without wavering, she spoke with moving sincerity.

"I can truthfully say to you that we children at home are full of cheerfulness and courage," she declared. "We are trying to do all we can to help our gallant sailors, soldiers, and airmen, and we are trying to bear our share of the danger and sadness of war."

Hitherto, if Princess Elizabeth had thought about queenship at all, her ideas had been those of any child daydreaming of being king or engine-driver. With the Windsor family, however, the focal interest of childhood days has always been horses rather than railway engines. A generation before, the previous heir to the Throne—"Uncle David"—had informed Lord Roberts that when he was King he would prevent "them" from using bearing reins on horses, as they were very cruel. The young Princess was reported by her governess as declaring: "If I am ever Queen I shall make a law that there must be no riding on Sundays. Horses should have a rest too. And I shan't let anyone dock their pony's tail."

With her broadcast of 1940, however, came the awakening

consciousness of the responsibility of her birthright, and there was a marked singleness of purpose about the way in which the young heiress presumptive applied herself to preparation for the destiny that lay ahead. Before a man or woman could make a good sovereign, he or she must first be a good citizen, and it was through youth movements, available and offering equal opportunity to all, that Princess Elizabeth learned in practice the elements of citizenship. On her own initiative she had joined the Girl Guides, a movement that she herself later described as "bounded by no narrow prejudice of race, class, or creed, but one seeking to join all together in friendship, based on a common promise and upon a common attempt to order their lives in accordance with the laws of the movement."

She had no greater facility for adhering to those laws or becoming proficient in Guide activities than any other girl of her age. In fact, so far as some of the practical activities were concerned, her position put her at a distinct disadvantage. Her Guide Captain recalls that the Princess, then fourteen, found considerable difficulty in passing the First Class Test.

"The Cook, Needlewoman, and Child Nurse are holding me up a bit, but I hope to pass soon," Princess Elizabeth explained, and added ruefully, "I think I have forgotten how to sweep a room now."

Years later Princess Elizabeth was to speak from personal knowledge of the difficulty of living constantly to the ideals of the movement when she addressed a conference of Rangers at Girl Guide Headquarters.

"The promise and laws are simple and anyone can understand them," she said, "but that does not make them easy to fulfil. On the contrary, they are difficult. They demand faith, honesty, self-control, and love for our neighbours. The demand that Rangers should hold to these high principles comes at one of the most difficult periods of their lives, when new emotions and new understanding often lead to doubt and delusion. Life today is a struggle. Rangers, in accepting their promise and the law, take upon themselves an extra struggle. They have to sacrifice themselves and keep their high ideals. If they do this successfully they will be greatly strengthened in a world that is full of materialism, dishonesty, and devotion to self."

With the approach of her sixteenth birthday, hopes began to be expressed that Princess Elizabeth should be created Princess of Wales. It was a wish that was to gain increasing support in the ensuing two years and culminate at the time of her eighteenth birthday in a widespread movement sponsored by the Welsh Parliamentary Party and many prominent Welsh figures and public authorities.

Since 1284 when, according to a popular legend of doubtful origin, Edward I gave his son, born in Caernarvon Castle, the title of "Prince of Wales" in fulfilment of a promise to give the Welsh people a Prince who could speak " no word of English," the title has been conferred with but one or two exceptions upon the Sovereign's eldest son.

The eldest son is automatically Duke of Cornwall by birth, but it is necessary for him to be created Prince of Wales. Whereas the dukedom of Cornwall was granted "to him (Edward II) and his heirs the first-begotten sons of the kings of England," the principality was conferred upon "him and his heirs the kings of England." Therefore upon the accession of a king who has been both Prince of Wales and Duke of Cornwall, the duchy of Cornwall will pass at once to his eldest son, but the principality of Wales remains the king's and is merged into the Crown without any separate entity until it is created anew.

If an heir apparent who is both Prince of Wales and Duke of Cornwall dies during the lifetime of the sovereign and leaves an heir, both titles lapse. His son cannot inherit them, for he is neither king of England nor "first-begotten son of a king of England." If, however, he had died childless and a brother had become heir to the throne, the dukedom would pass to the brother as the heir and living first-begotten son of the king.

In the case where a king has no son, the dukedom of Cornwall remains in abeyance until the son of a sovereign is born. There has, of course, been a recent example of this. Upon his mother's accession, Prince Charles, as the eldest son of the Sovereign, became automatically Duke of Cornwall and revived the title that had lapsed with the accession of Edward VIII. It is for the Queen to decide if and when he shall be created Prince of Wales.

In the first flush of fatherhood Henry VIII did give his first child, Mary, the title of Princess of Wales, although he subsequently took it away from her after his divorce from her mother, Catherine of Aragon, and marriage to Anne Boleyn. Apart from this temporary deviation, which could hardly be regarded as a precedent, the Prince of Wales, for over six hundred years, has continued to be the heir apparent to the throne.

By reason of her sex Princess Elizabeth could never be heir apparent. She was heiress presumptive; that is, it was presumed that she would succeed to the throne provided no male birth intervened to displace her from the succession. Even when such an intervention was beyond all bounds of physical possibility, she would remain heiress presumptive. Had her aunt, Princess Mary, not been alive, there is no doubt that Princess Elizabeth would have been made the Princess Royal, a title, Prussian in origin, which was first borrowed by George II for his eldest daughter.

In the case of the other queens regnant the position, so far as the Principality of Wales was concerned, had been somewhat different. Mary I had succeeded her brother, Edward VI, and had been followed by her sister Elizabeth. Mary II was, it is true, placed on the throne as joint sovereign with her husband William of Orange (William III) after her father, James II, was deposed, but this was no normal succession. Anne succeeded her brother-in-law, William III, and the Crown came to Victoria from her uncle, William IV. Of all our queens regnant our present Queen was the first to follow her father in direct natural succession to the throne.

This directness of natural succession, coupled with the fact that the likelihood of a royal brother was becoming more and more remote, seemed to many to make it pointless to deprive Wales of a royal leader and Princess Elizabeth of an honour that would have received universal acclaim. British monarchy, however, is an institution that thinks not in terms of ten or twenty years, but in generations. A precedent now might be an embarrassment in years to come, and so from Buckingham Palace on February 11th, 1944, came the announcement that "His Majesty the King does not contemplate making any change in the style and title of the Princess Elizabeth on the occasion of her approaching eighteenth birthday."

It was no doubt in sympathy with the popular viewpoint, however, that King George VI selected South Wales as the first area to which Princess Elizabeth should accompany him and the Queen on an official tour, and the people of Wales made up for any disappointment at the lack of the official title by hailing her unofficially as "Ein Tywysoges" (Our own Princess).

On March 28th, 1942, Princess Elizabeth was confirmed by the Archbishop of Canterbury in the private chapel of Windsor Castle. She was within a month of her sixteenth birthday. Only two years were left before the Princess would have to be ready, if necessary, to assume the Crown and the leadership of her people without notice.

Years before, in one of the first speeches he ever made as Duke of York, her father had spoken of his ideas of leadership. To his mind, the leader needed three great qualities: personality, sympathy, and, above all, idealism.

"I do not think I need speak to you about personality," he said. "Of sympathy I will say just this: its keynote is personal contact and understanding. The third quality of the leader is idealism. Nobody can lead unless he has the gift of vision, and the desire in his soul to leave things in the world a little better than he found them. He will strive for something which may be unattainable, but which he believes in his heart can one day be reached. If not by him, by his successors, if he can help pave the way."

King George VI had striven always to imbue and develop personality and idealism in his daughter by her daily routine of living, by her solid family atmosphere, by his own example, by his "helping to pave the way for his successors"—in particular, his daughter—towards the goal of a better life in a better world.

Now, at an age when she could responsibly enter into the Church with appreciation of the obligation entailed, it was time also to begin the personal contact of future leader and subject, and the development of the quality of understanding and sympathy. As a first step the heiress presumptive was officially introduced to the armed forces by her appointment as Colonel of the Grenadier Guards. The Grenadiers are the first of the five regiments—the others are the Coldstream, and the Scots, Irish, and Welsh Guards—which constitute the Brigade of Guards.

Thrilled by the appointment—her first under the Crown, and one unique in the respect that it was the first time in their history that the Grenadiers had a woman as their colonel—the sixteen-year-old Princess tackled her duties with an enthusiasm and thoroughness that were at first inclined to be over-zealous, for she did not appreciate the repercussions that were likely to follow her frankly expressed criticisms, and the fact that one of the qualities of a good officer was the ability to temper judgment with mercy.

Her appointment was not an honorary one. When the Guards were formed during the Protectorate in 1656 by Charles II from amongst his supporters in exile, the first colonel, the Earl of Wentworth, found that he had insufficient time to devote to his regimental duties. He therefore appointed a lieutenant-colonel to act as deputy in his absence. Since then the colonels of the five regiments have been either members of the royal family or figures of outstanding military distinction, and the commanding officers, whilst holding the full rank of a colonel, have always been known as the "Lieutenant-Colonel Commanding." The colonel-in-chief of each of the five regiments and supreme commander of the brigade as a whole has always been the reigning sovereign.

For ten years Princess Elizabeth was to serve as Colonel of the Grenadiers, until the death of her father and her accession as sovereign required her to assume the role of Colonel-in-Chief and relinquish the rank that had been her first appointment under the Crown. With a touch of sadness and regret she bade farewell to her regiment at a parade arranged at her special request on her twenty-sixth birthday.

"I shall never hear the 'British Grenadiers,' " she said, referring to the regimental march, "without a stirring of my heart and a feeling of pride and comradeship."

In addition to reviewing her Grenadiers and receiving from them the present of a diamond brooch in the form of the regimental badge, Princess Elizabeth had one other public duty to perform on her sixteenth birthday—the duty that fell to all of her age no matter how high or humble their birth. In girl guide uniform she attended at the Windsor Employment Exchange and registered in the normal way as a private citizen for national service.

A well-known photographer remarked once of the difficulty he experienced in composing group portraits of the royal family because of their instinctive and almost unbreakable habit of "standing in line." If ever Princess Elizabeth felt tempted to break out of line, it was over the question of national service. Throughout history that martial spark has ever been within the make-up of our sovereign queens, ready to flame into action when danger threatened. Queen Victoria in her yacht, *Fairy*, led her Fleet out of harbour on their way to do battle in the Baltic during the Crimean War. When she instituted the Victoria Cross as the supreme award for valour in action she exulted in the thought that at her investiture "the rough hand of the brave and honest private soldier came for the first time in contact with that of his Sovereign and Queen!"

Queen Anne fought at home to sustain Marlborough's campaign against the French which, with the victories of Blenheim, Ramillies, Oudenarde, and Malplaquet, wrote probably the greatest chapter in British military history. Mary I—the "Bloody Mary" of the schoolboy history books—for all the weaknesses and misfortunes of her reign, had no qualms about rallying her supporters and riding at their head on London to claim her Crown from the usurper, Northumberland, and his unfortunate puppet, Lady Jane Grey.

And, greatest of all, our Queen's own namesake, the first Elizabeth, united with a woman's wiles and strategy a nation impoverished and divided against itself, and built up a national pride and strength able at last to meet with force the might of Spain.

"I know I have the body of a weak and feeble woman, but I have the heart and stomach of a king, and a king of England, too," she proclaimed as she rode bareheaded amongst her soldiers at Tilbury where, should Howard of Effingham and Drake fail to intercept the Spanish Armada, the army of which she had appointed herself commander-in-chief stood ready to defend her realm. "And think foul scorn that Parma or Spain, or any prince of Europe, should dare to invade the borders of my realm; to which, rather than any dishonour shall grow by me, I myself will take up arms, I myself will be your general, judge, and rewarder of every one of your virtues in the field."

Elizabeth the First may have scorned the "weak and feeble body of a woman" that kept her from the battle arena proper, but for Elizabeth the Second time and notions had changed.

No longer conscious of any handicap of sex, the emancipated woman was taking her place side by side with her brother-in-arms, sustaining hardship, discomfort, and danger with the same fortitude as he did, and as with many a young man and woman under age or in a reserved occupation, Princess Elizabeth's one desire was to enlist as quickly as possible.

Both King and Cabinet, however, considered that un-interrupted training for the throne was her most vital form of national service and must outweigh all other considerations. It was not a decision that the Princess found easy to accept, and she continued to use all her powers of persuasion to have it reversed.

In her case, too, the desire to serve in His Majesty's Forces was not confined to a personal satisfaction of the impulsive patriotism of youth. Princess Elizabeth's was the generation upon whom the fulfilment of the eventual victory would de-pend. It would be she who would ultimately lead her contem-poraries in the rebuilding of peace and the fashioning of the future. To share the same wartime experiences as girls of her own age would, she considered, be an invaluable asset to her understanding of her future subjects and their problems.

It was this argument, no doubt, that ultimately prevailed and led to the reversal of the original decision. On March 4th, 1945, it was announced that:

"The King has granted Her Royal Highness the Princess Elizabeth a commission with the honorary rank of second subaltern in the Auxiliary Territorial Service. Her Royal High-ness is at present attending a course at a driving training centre in the south of England."

It must have been with pride that King George VI signed his daughter's commission. Although at first he had opposed this course, he must privately have had every sympathy with her wish. He knew himself what it was to chafe at State considerations of security and safety that kept him tied to his island realm when he would sooner have been leading his Forces in action. As it was, he was visiting them in Gibraltar, North Africa, and Italy at the first possible opportunity, and he made up his mind that he was going to witness the opening of the Second Front.

That he agreed to waive the idea was as much a compromise to keep out of danger his Prime Minister, who had intended to sail with a cruiser squadron. In the fifth volume of his war memoirs Mr. Churchill reproduces a copy of a letter King George VI wrote to him from Buckingham Palace on June 2nd, 1944:

"I am a younger man than you," the King pointed out. "I am a sailor, and as King I am the Head of all these Services. There is nothing I would like better than to go to sea, but I have agreed to stay at home: is it fair that you should then do exactly what I should have liked to do myself?

"You said yesterday afternoon that it would be a fine thing for the King to lead his troops into battle, as in old days; if the King cannot do this, it does not seem to me right that his Prime Minister should take his place."

Even so, on June 17th, 1944, within a fortnight of D-Day, King George VI was visiting his own and Allied troops in Normandy.

Like father, like daughter. At the A.T.S. Mechanical Transport Training Centre near Camberley, King's daughter and Colonel of the Grenadier Guards was entered in the records as "No. 230873 Second Subaltern Elizabeth Alexandra Mary Windsor. Age 18. Eyes, blue. Hair, brown. Height, 5 ft. 3 in. National Registration Number: SWGC 55/1/."

There, on the express instructions of the King and at her

own personal wish, Princess Elizabeth was treated exactly the same as any other trainee of second subaltern rank. In addition to studying military law and administration, she learned the Service method of driving and maintaining small cars, heavy lorries, and ambulances. Maintenance included the regular routine of overhauling, cleaning and greasing, topping-up batteries, adjustment of carburettor, the changing of wheels and plugs, and the taking down and reassembling of an internal-combustion engine. By the time she had finished the course, the heiress presumptive had driven in convoys, and in an end-of-term, high-spirited gesture she drove her instructor via Piccadilly Circus and London's streets of heaviest traffic from Camberley to Buckingham Palace.

The training report on the newly-qualified royal transport officer stated: "Extremely quick to learn. She is not rash and drives with consideration and thought for others on the road, and with every care for her car."

There was one other experience that Princess Elizabeth gained during her A.T.S. days, an understanding that will remain with her long after the memory of differentials and gearboxes has faded. During her training, first her aunt, the Princess Royal, then the King and Queen arrived to inspect her unit; and she gained an unexpected insight into the bustle of preparation and polish that precedes the arrival of royalty.

"I have never seen a royal visit from the inside before," she commented. "I did not know so much preparation went on."

At her lessons

Studio Lisa

Associated Press

Leaving for a concert

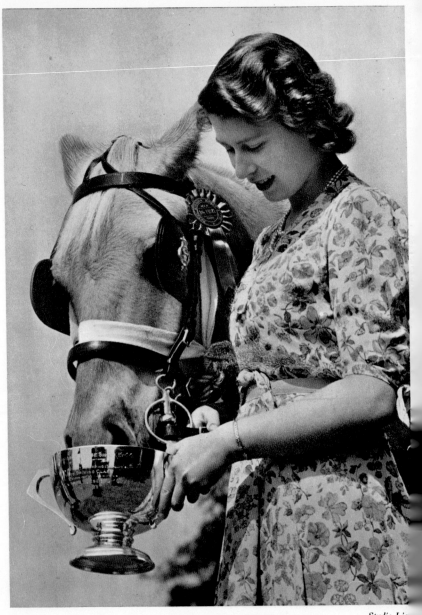

At Windsor Castle, May 1944

8

"I SERVE"

ALTHOUGH the aura of family unity which now surrounds the throne has been a particular development of recent years, the Crown has always been a family service—or "family firm" as King George VI once described it. Even today the immediate members of the royal family are precluded from entering the professional or commercial worlds, or engaging in any activity for profit. They are required to devote their lives to public service, supporting, and deputising for the Crown itself.

The family service upon which the throne has been built is not restricted to kings and queens; it applies equally to the servants of sovereigns. Just as the Crown has passed from father to son, brother to brother, uncle to niece, mother to son, father to daughter, so have appointments in the royal household run in families for generations. In the two years from sixteen to eighteen that the King's daughter and heiress began training in earnest for her allotted role, so the sons and daughters of the King's servants trained for the positions they would take up in Princess Elizabeth's own household. In Windsor Great Park, at a special training school established more than a hundred years ago by Queen Victoria, they studied housecraft, cooking, gardening, needlework, and general domestic subjects, while their future mistress began to emerge in public, accompanying her father and mother on royal tours and visits to war factories, the Services, civil defence units, civic centres, and public utility undertakings.

At eighteen Princess Elizabeth was granted her own coat of arms—the Royal Arms of England labelled with a Tudor Rose between two crosses of St. George. The incorporation of the White Rose of York—the first time it had been used in this manner—was the King's own idea: a reference to the days when he had been Duke, and his daughter Princess, of the House of York. At eighteen, too, she began to make public appearances without her parents.

Much as Princess Elizabeth may have liked to do so, it was not feasible that the heiress presumptive should remain isolated in some settled sphere of A.T.S. activity. The nation as a whole wanted to see her; and it was important that she should extend her personal contact with people both in support of her father and in training for her future queenship. The period of service in the A.T.S. had to be limited. Once its purpose had been accomplished, the heiress presumptive could no longer be spared from State duties. Refreshed by the complete change of environment and occupation that the A.T.S. life had afforded her, she returned with renewed vigour to public life on an increasing scale.

She returned, too, with a consciousness of benefit and development that she was later to recall at a reunion of ex-Service women.

"I am sure," she said, "that each one of us gained something, and most of us a great deal, from our service with the Colours. The rough, no less than the smooth, gave us a chance to develop qualities which should make us better wives, mothers, and citizens. Perhaps, above all, we should be proud of belonging to a body which, in days when far too many worship at the shrine of material advantage, has always put service to the community as the first of its ideals."

Between May 1944, when she made her first public speech— a simple reply to her election as President of the Queen Elizabeth Hospital for Children, the hospital of which her mother had laid the foundation-stone—and her enlistment in the A.T.S., Princess Elizabeth fulfilled some dozen or so official engagements by herself.

The most important of these was the launching on December 1st, 1944, of Britain's biggest battleship, H.M.S. *Vanguard*. For the first time Princess Elizabeth's own standard was broken from a flagstaff, and it blew out bravely in a bitter December wind over the massed crowds of Clydeside shipbuilders and their families and neighbours. On the way to the platform one of the officials in the party commented on the cold weather, but the Princess replied: "I'm too nervous to notice it."

There was nothing nervous, however, about the ringing tones in which she proclaimed: "I name this ship *Vanguard*. God bless her and all who sail in her."

The bottle of Empire wine shattered against the prow in the ritual christening, but the ship remained motionless. Between the pressing of the button operating the launching mechanism and the movement of the ship there was a time-lag of several seconds, and for a moment the eighteen-years-old Princess showed a glimpse of her inward nervousness.

"Oh dear," she whispered to Mr. A. V. Alexander, then First Lord of the Admiralty, "she isn't going to move."

Her concern was needless, however. Almost as she expressed her fear, the ship slid slowly down the slipway into the water to the shouts and cheering of the crowd and the crashing chords of "Rule Britannia," and Princess Elizabeth smiled with relief.

Three hundred and fifty-six years before, the first *Vanguard*, a small wooden galleon riding low in the water, had set sail with the Fleet of little ships raised by the untiring efforts of the first Queen Elizabeth to defend her realm against the Spanish Armada. Since then seven other *Vanguards* had spanned the years in a serial saga of Britain's naval history. It was in a *Vanguard* that Nelson had defeated the French at the Battle of the Nile.

Now, by the grace of God, this forty-thousand-tons battleship, ninth ship of the line to bear the name *Vanguard*, was to escape world war and come instead into commission for the peaceful pursuit of carrying Their Majesties and the Princess to South Africa in February 1947.

Even as Princess Elizabeth launched the ship, however, it was generally accepted that, biggest and mightiest of battleships that she was, *Vanguard* would probably be the last of her type. In the matter of the months that she had been under construction, wartime experiences had rendered her almost obsolete. The chapter on battleships was in its last pages. It belonged to the first part of the twentieth century, to the reigns of the Princess's father and grandfather. Now, as she herself unknowingly approached the throne, the battleship was finally yielding place to the aircraft carrier, and within fifteen months Princess Elizabeth was sailing to Belfast to launch the newest and latest aircraft carrier, *Eagle*, the ship that would incorporate all the results of the 1939-45 war and come into commission as Her Majesty's Ship *Eagle*, pride of her Navy.

Ships of wood, ships of steel, ships with wings—from the first Elizabeth to the second Elizabeth outward appearances have altered, but the "hearts of oak"—"powerful, tough and hardy, the product of many centuries of slow and steady growth," to use Princess Elizabeth's own description of the English tree—remain an unchanged symbol of both our naval and national characteristics.

So interwoven are our national and maritime histories—as King George VI said when he opened the National Maritime Museum at Greenwich in 1937, "but for the enterprise, the knowledge, and the character of our seamen the British Commonwealth of Nations would never have come into existence"—that it is not surprising that the Princess, daughter of a sailor king, inherited a deep love of the sea. Among the engagements and invitations that began to flood upon her she looked gladly upon those that had to do with the sea. With equal pride and delight she would launch liner and oil-tanker or attend any occasion with the Navy, from which she was to choose her husband and which she regarded not only as "the first guardian and bulwark of our islands" but "guardian of liberty throughout the world, a comforter of the oppressed, and a sword against tyrants."

Britain's maritime history was as magnificent and stirring to Princess Elizabeth as it was to any who inherited the tradition of Nelson and Drake, and she looked to the time when she would be contributing her own instalment to the saga, not with the powder and smoke of her famous namesake but with the sea itself as the sole and sufficient challenge to the island spirit of adventure.

"The story of our greatness at sea," she said when she opened a new wing at the Greenwich Museum, "is surely one which will keep alive in our hearts the very qualities which give it greatness. I hope it will, for the story is not yet ended. The sea which surrounds our island and which separates yet binds together the different parts of the Commonwealth, still presents a challenge to our courage and our inventive genius, and many chapters of the story of our maritime history—I hope peaceful ones—remain to be written by us and our children."

It was natural that prominent also amongst the engagements of those first years of public service should figure matters affecting the younger generation, whose leader Princess Elizabeth was. She presided over committees, she opened clubs, she reviewed parades, and as the war ended she turned her attention more and more to youth welfare and interests, and to inspiring youth to rebuild and plan for the future that would belong to her and to her contemporaries. Never before, she realised, had the country been so much in need of courage and high purpose.

Inevitably the problems of youth arose from conditions in the home, from homes shattered by the war and its consequences, by broken marriages and domestic strife, by lack of discipline and morals, by cruelty and neglect.

She to whom the words "home" and "family" were synonymous with unity and love, strength and security, could not understand how anyone could be cruel to a child. One of her first presidencies was that of the National Society for the Prevention of Cruelty to Children.

"To be cruel to a little child is indeed a dreadful crime," she told one of the society's meetings in 1945. "It is sad to reflect that in these days there should be need for a society such as ours, but there can be no doubt as to its value to the whole community. Now the war in Europe is won and we can look forward to peace in the future, I trust it will be possible for our society to devote its full powers to give every child a chance to lead a happy and useful life."

And again she expressed her Society's aim: "A good home

life is the rock on which a child's future is founded. It is, therefore, the aim of the society to keep the family united and to remove, wherever possible, all that might injure children either mentally or physically."

Constantly the Princess exhorted the different youth organisations—the organisations of which she had had personal experience and to which she looked to provide the backbone of citizenship amongst her future subjects—to fear not the adventurous path that lay ahead, but to meet it with courage and resourcefulness and make it a path that would lead to a way of peace, new life, and happiness. That way, however, could come from no splendid isolation. One of the good things that had come out of the war was international friendship, and at a time when the government was regarding foreign travel as a luxury that we were unable to afford, Princess Elizabeth was fearlessly advocating the maintenance of those wartime friendships by the interchange of visits by schools and youth organisations.

"We must accept responsibility of building together with citizens of other nations a strong framework for a world where all men should have freedom of belief and thought. Let us take it up with courage and determination, keeping faith with those who, by their strength and sacrifice, handed the future into our keeping," she declared. Later, when she received the honorary degree of doctor of laws at Edinburgh University, she summed up her views: "Travel and freedom to study the lives and thoughts of others are the surest guarantees against tyranny. Indeed, I doubt whether any country which has closed its doors to ideas from abroad has ever flourished or remained truly civilised."

It is often recorded, though on doubtful authority, that

Queen Victoria said in the early days of her reign: "They wished to treat me like a girl, but I will show them that I am Queen of England." The attitude, anyway, was typical of her first approach to sovereignty, and one, springing from in-experience combined with a youthful impulsiveness and obstinacy, that was to lead her into unconstitutional acts.

There was nothing during those apprentice years of Princess Elizabeth to suggest that she would be liable to repeat the mistakes of her great-great-grandmother, but there was everything to indicate that the future queen had an emphatic mind of her own. Although there was no doubt that her thorough training and natural instinct would steer her clear of constitutional error, it was equally obvious that if Princess Elizabeth felt deeply that a thing needed saying, she would say it frankly without pulling any punches. She would not be content with making the perfunctory speech that custom expected of royalty.

The aftermath of war had made apparent the general apathy towards morals and religion. It had brought also a diffidence at voicing personal criticism of this trend, however much one may in one's heart have condemned it. The fashion for deriding the basic principles of our code of living was too strong for the average citizen, particularly the younger members of the community, to make an open stand against it.

Wise leadership, Princess Elizabeth considered, could ultimately change this blasé and materialistic outlook, and as she was the hereditary leader of the post-war generation she had no qualms about fearlessly giving a lead in forthright criticism. She referred to the subject on numerous occasions, but never more forcibly than on October 18th, 1949, when she made to a rally of young wives organised by the Mothers' Union what, apart from her coming-of-age broadcast, has probably been her most memorable and important speech.

"I would go so far as to say that some of the very principles on which the family, and therefore the health of the nation, is founded are in danger," Princess Elizabeth uncompromisingly declared. "Even if we can allow for the rosy hue in which the passage of years sometimes colours the past, we can hardly help admitting that we live in an age of growing self-indulgence, of hardening materialism, and of falling moral standards. There will always be unhappy marriages, especially when, as in time of war and of housing shortages, it is difficult for people to live normal married lives. But when we see around us the havoc which has been wrought, above all among children, by the break-up of homes, we can have no doubt that divorce and separation are responsible for some of the darkest evils in our society today.

"I do not think you can perform any finer service than to help maintain the Christian doctrine that the relation of husband and wife is a permanent one, not lightly to be broken because of difficulties or quarrels. . . . I believe there is a far greater fear in our generation of being labelled as priggish. In consequence, people are sometimes afraid to show disapproval of what they know to be wrong, and thus they end by seeming to condone what in their hearts they dislike. I am sure that it is just as wrong to err on that side as it is to be intolerant and over-critical."

Reproduced, commented upon, and discussed throughout the world, this speech drew from Britain's most powerful ally the following tribute in a leading article in the *New York Herald Tribune*:

"We like to think she showed a very human unwillingness

to stay within the bounds of the merely gracious and formal speech that British tradition usually imposes on royalty. She spoke as might any serious young leader who finds all is not right with the world, of divorce rate and evils that attend broken homes. It takes a woman with a far more than normal poise, courage, and independent mind to emerge as a distinct, let alone decisive personality from the role prescribed for a Princess in Britain's almost entirely symbolic royalty.

"After this speech many British folk will be saying that Princess Elizabeth is like Queen Victoria. They will approve and heed her forceful little sermon—not only because what she said was right and sensible, but because her saying it suggests that the young woman who will one day be Queen has ideas of her own."

The same practical, realistic outlook marked Princess Elizabeth's approach to post-war conditions generally. If ever people had believed that the end of the war would bring an end to austerity they were quickly disillusioned. In the immediate need and urgency of the moment the imperative problem of the struggle for existence had overridden all other considerations. We had lived on capital and credit and there had been neither time nor desire to consider the reckoning. Our reserves and the income from them had vanished in the flames. We were no longer banker of the world, and we had no power to resume the role. We had not even the means to sustain our own domestic economy, let alone invest a surplus for revenue from abroad. With the savings of generations exhausted and our resources mortgaged to the hilt, we had to awaken to the grim, chilling realisation of crushing debts combined with empty larder and empty purse. Britain had to start afresh, from scratch, to earn her living and her place amongst the free peoples of the world; and with the switch from war to peace had also to come the change from budgeting for the present alone. Though we could provide barely sufficient for a hand-to-mouth existence, we had to start setting aside reserves and rebuilding for the future.

Austerity was, indeed, not only the order of the day but the outlook for years to come. The spacious days of her great-great-grandmother, which could afford a solid workmanship and products built to endure for all their lack of the elegance that typified the Augustan age of yet another Queen, Anne, were not to be the inheritance of the second Elizabeth.

The heiress presumptive was unperturbed. With a crusading fire of youthful enthusiasm she sought in austerity itself the challenge against which the nation could match its inherent spirit of adventure. This was no time for regrets. A defeatist attitude bemoaning shortages and existing conditions, and using them as an excuse for the inferior, would get us nowhere. If we did lack some of the facilities and resources of our fathers, then we must concentrate upon what was available and utilise those assets not just to make do, but to pioneer in new trends and spheres.

In this crusade she sought the assistance of the Royal Society of Arts, when she addressed them in November 1947.

"It may well be long years before we can afford to devote such leisure and energy to things purely decorative as did our forefathers," Princess Elizabeth said. "But we should be defeatist and unimaginative indeed if we concluded that because nearly everything we produce today must be severely practical it must also be without taste or beauty.

"Great Britain led the world into the industrial revolution. That was no doubt an historic contribution to human progress, but there has also been a legacy of squalor, misery, and ugliness as well as the fall in standards of taste which accompanied mass-production. In a sense, we have a duty to lead the world in finding the remedy. If we are destined to live in an austere age, it is for us to establish that beauty is as essential to utility as it is proverbially to truth."

9

THE CROWN TODAY

ONCE when someone commented upon the strenuous-
ness of a tour that Princess Elizabeth had undertaken,
she replied: "At times like that you just have to forget about
feeling tired."

Living constantly in the full glare of the spotlight with every
trait, every emotion, every human failing, thrown up harshly
in black and white, royalty knows no shadows or half-tones.
Members of the royal family can never relax. They can never
put their feet up. They can afford no minor indiscretion or indulgence that in any other mortal would be taken as a matter
of course. There can be no deviation from the strict, narrow,
sometimes hidebound path that has been carved for them.
There is no limit to the intimate details of their lives that become the automatic subject for comment and criticism by an
audience of over five hundred million people scattered throughout the countries of the British Commonwealth of Nations.
Even the innermost privacy of the heart does not escape this
searching scrutiny.

Long before the full burden of the Crown was to descend
upon her, Princess Elizabeth had discovered that any attempt
to share the normal recreations and pleasures of her own generation could be made only at the cost of the inevitable public
post-mortem. If she went to a party, whom she danced with,
what she drank, the hour at which she returned home—every
personal item would be noted, reported, repeated. To this

77

intrusion into her personal leisure the Princess became inured. She accepted, too, the fact that she had only to dance once with an eligible male for his name to be mentioned as her possible husband. At first there may have been an instinctive reaction of indignation at these unfounded match-making reports and rumours, but as she became accustomed to the inevitable, the ever-growing list of names coupled with hers began to amuse her.

It was natural, of course, that people should be interested in, and wonder about, the man who would be husband of their future queen, but provided he was not a Roman Catholic they would have no legal say in the matter. True, the people in the person of the Prime Minister had brought their opinion to bear in the case of King Edward VIII, but then they had some justification in the fact that whomever he married would automatically be their Queen. Whomsoever Princess Elizabeth married would never be their king, but only husband of the Queen, an entirely domestic role with no official rights or powers in the government of the country.

When Philip of Spain married the first Queen of England, Mary I, he did so with the intention of being crowned king and bringing the country under Spanish domination. The nation, however, had taken every safeguard to thwart any such ambitions and had left him without authority or influence in English affairs. In these precautions parliament set a precedent that has continued ever since. It is one, too, in keeping with the practice throughout all classes of society that a man raises his wife to his own status, but cannot conversely be raised to her level if she is of higher rank than he. Not unnaturally when the Duke of Edinburgh appeared on the left of Princess Elizabeth in the wedding portraits, this reversal of the customary placing of bride on bridegroom's left was widely attributed to the Princess's precedence; but the real reason was that the Duke was in naval uniform wearing a sword and walked on the left of his bride because he did not wish to damage her dress.

Whether Mary I followed her brother, Edward, to the throne by reason of the fact that no male offspring of a sovereign remained to claim the throne and she was the eldest living daughter of Henry VIII, or by right of conquest over Northumberland and Lady Jane Grey, is an open question. An outcome of the feudal system had been the development of the principle of primogeniture in which the eldest son was established as sole heir, so that the property and power therefrom remained intact within the family instead of being shared and ultimately disintegrating. Only in the case where a man died leaving no son did the sharing of his estate apply. Where there was no son as heir, the inheritance did not pass intact to the eldest daughter, but was shared by her as a coparcener with her sisters.

Gradually the principle of primogeniture was applied also to the succession to the throne. It was a slow evolution from the elective system of the Witenagemot of Anglo-Saxon days, and did not come suddenly into our history like the formulation of a new law. In fact, in the fourteenth and fifteenth centuries the struggles between the Houses of York and Lancaster often caused any hereditary right to yield place to the mightier argument of conquest. Not until the Act of Settlement in 1701 was a qualified hereditary succession finally established by law.

The first attempt by a woman to claim the throne upon her father's death had been made by Matilda, the daughter of Henry I, who died in 1135 leaving no son. She could not, however, find sufficient support for the view that, by reason of being the sovereign's eldest child, the Crown was hers as a matter of right, and she was excluded in favour of Stephen, grandson of William the Conqueror by his daughter Adela. Subsequently Matilda's claim to the throne divided the country, although supporters rallied to her cause more from personal motives than from any desire to uphold a legal principle. Strife between the two factions continued intermittently for eighteen years before the Treaty of Wallingford finally settled the dispute on the terms that Stephen should continue to reign for his lifetime, after which the Crown should pass to Matilda's son, Henry, who became Henry II, the first of the Plantagenet kings.

Though Matilda failed in the struggle to gain the Crown for herself, she had at least paved the way for our own Queen Elizabeth to reign over us. In acknowledging a woman's right to the throne England was one of the few exceptions. Most countries followed what is known as the Salic Law, although no such doctrine is in fact found amongst the Salic laws, which were primarily a table of punishments drawn up by the Franks, the Germanic race from which France derived its name.

England first showed support for the view that a woman could inherit a right to a throne when the main line of the Capets, the dynasty of French kings, died out in 1328. Through his mother, Isabella, who was daughter of the French king, Philip IV, Edward III laid claim to the throne of France. To counter this the French declared that both females and their male heirs and successors were excluded from the throne, and the son of Charles of Valois was promptly crowned as Philip VI. Presumably to give the weight of antiquity to this decision, the French cited this ruling as the thousand-years-old Salic Law.

Years later this same Salic Law divided the thrones of Britain and Hanover, which had been united under the Act of Settlement in the person of George I. When William IV died, Queen

Training in the A.T.S., 1945

The late King with his stamp collection, December 1944

In her sitting-room at Buckingham Palace, 1946

Victoria succeeded him to the throne of Britain but, as a woman, was debarred from succession to that of Hanover. The nearest male heir, who was Victoria's uncle, Ernest, Duke of Cumberland, accordingly became King of Hanover. Britain benefited rather than suffered from this separation by her freedom from an entanglement which might have dragged the country into the Austro-Prussian war over the division of the Schleswig-Holstein territory that had been ceded by Denmark to the Confederation of German States in 1864. As it was, Prussia, with Italy's support, was overwhelmingly victorious. Hanover, which had supported the Austrians, was annexed by Prussia and the king deposed.

Throughout history, the disputation of female rights in the succession to thrones has ever been a convenient peg on which to justify action to suit prevailing individual interests. Even Kaiser Wilhelm II, for all the Germanic upholding of the Salic Law, was not above proclaiming his right to the throne of Britain on the grounds that he was the son of Queen Victoria's first child, the Princess Royal, who married Emperor Frederick of Prussia.

It was ostensibly in support of his claim to the French throne, but doubtless also with an eye to profitable booty from a hated enemy, that Edward III invaded France in 1339 and began the Hundred Years War. In the latter part of the struggle, Henry V as well was to make much play of his claim through Edward III and Isabella to the French Crown.

By the time that Mary Tudor came on the scene, therefore, her succession was generally accepted to be a matter of right, notwithstanding the fact that she had to take up arms to foil the plot of a usurper and gain her throne. Those who subsequently rebelled against her did so entirely on political and religious grounds, and had Mary been overthrown they would have crowned another woman, Henry VIII's second daughter Elizabeth, as their sovereign a little before her natural time.

Only in the case of Mary II and William III has the queen's husband been crowned king and enthroned as joint sovereign, and in that instance the circumstances were revolutionary. With the deposition of James II the normal succession was broken, and the passing of the Crown once again reverted to the elective character of the Anglo-Saxon system. It was with the full knowledge and approval of the majority of parliament and people that the offer of the Crown was made jointly to James's daughter and her husband. Even so, steps were taken to exclude from the succession any heirs William might have by a wife other than Mary.

In the case of our last queen regnant there is no denying that when Albert married Victoria he was more in love with the position he imagined the marriage would bring him than he was with his bride, to whom he referred (amongst his intimate friends) as "our beloved aunt." He discovered quickly that the position of queen's husband meant nothing and, with government and politics virtually a closed door to him, had to seek outlet for his frustrated energies in the domestic reorganisation of the royal household and then in spurring national trade and commerce through his own brain-child, the Great Exhibition of 1851.

From his experience Albert set down this opinion on the role of queen's consort:

"While a female sovereign has a great many disadvantages in comparison with a king, yet if she is married and her husband understands and does his duty, her position on the other hand has its many compensating advantages, and in the long run will be found even to be stronger than that of a male sovereign.

"But this requires that the husband should entirely sink his own *individual* existence in that of his wife: that he should aim at no power by himself or for himself: should shun all contention, assume no separate responsibility before the public, but make his position entirely a part of hers: fill up every gap which, as a woman, she would naturally leave in the exercise of her regal functions: continually and anxiously watch every part of public business in order to be able to advise and assist her at any moment in any of the multifarious and difficult questions or duties brought before her, sometimes international, sometimes political, social, or personal."

Under the Royal Marriages Act of 1772, no member of the royal family "male or female (other than the issue of Princesses who have married or who may marry into foreign families) shall be capable of contracting matrimony without the previous consent of His Majesty, his heirs, and successors, signified under the Great Seal." If the sovereign refuses consent and the royal person concerned is over twenty-five years of age, then he or she may give notice to the Privy Council and the marriage may take place after twelve months provided parliament has not meanwhile expressed disapproval.

The meeting of the Privy Council augmented by the presence of Commonwealth representatives which was convened by the King after he had given his consent to his daughter's betrothal was called solely to receive the news, and not for the purpose of giving any sanction to the match. In the national interest it was of course extremely desirable that the man whom the heiress presumptive chose should be not only popular in this country but meet also with the unqualified approbation of the Commonwealth nations. The restless, post-war years of uncertainty made it particularly vital that the strength and personality of the Crown, the one link that could hold together the British Commonwealth of Nations against the forces of adversity, should continue unimpaired.

Whilst the rumours of her choice remained unfounded and guesses were wide of the mark, they left Princess Elizabeth un-scathed. It was when love ripened and her secret was prema-turely discovered that she knew the full pillory of her position. For all her royal birth, she was still a young woman with all the natural reserve and sensitiveness of a girl very much in love, but where royalty is concerned no emotion is sacred. Sometimes it must have taken all her royal training and self-control to retain her composure and mask the embarrassment and pain in her heart caused by the shouts of "Philip!" that the crowd thoughtlessly hurled at her at a time when nothing was official and the Palace was still repudiating published reports with the guarded statement: "Princess Elizabeth is not engaged to be married."

It was on March 18th, 1947, that amongst a list of British naturalisations published in the *London Gazette* appeared the entry: "Mountbatten, Philip; Greece; serving officer in His Majesty's Forces; 16 Chester Street, London, S.W.1." Prince Philip of Greece and Denmark had taken the oath of allegiance on February 28th of that year, and under the normal procedure abandoned his foreign titles to become Lieutenant Philip Mountbatten, R.N.

He had made his first application for naturalisation in 1939, but before this could go through war intervened and all naturalisation was suspended. At the end of the war, in which he received a Mention in Despatches for his service as a mid-

Associated Press

Receiving a twenty-first birthday present at Government House, Salisbury,
Rhodesia, 1947

A visit to the diamond mines at Kimberley, South Africa

shipman in H.M.S. *Valiant* at the Battle of Cape Matapan, he availed himself of the priority application for naturalisation available to all aliens who had served with distinction in His Majesty's Forces. His papers were submitted through the proper channels of his commanding officer and the Board of Admiralty.

Like his bride-to-be, Philip Mountbatten was a great-great-grandchild of Queen Victoria, from whom he was descended on the maternal side through her second daughter, Princess Alice. Princess Alice's daughter married the first Marquis of Milford Haven, and their eldest daughter, sister of Admiral Viscount Mountbatten of Burma, became the wife of Prince Andrew, youngest son of King George I of Greece, who was assassinated in 1913. Although King of Greece, Philip's parental grandfather—the brother of our Queen Alexandra—had no Greek blood in him: he was the son of Christian IX of Denmark, and was appointed to the vacant throne of the Hellenes at the request of the Greeks in 1867. As neither the royal families of Greece nor Denmark bear any House name, there was no surname on his father's side for Prince Philip to assume on renouncing his title and becoming a commoner. He therefore adopted that of his mother's family, Mountbatten.

Educated in Britain, he went to the Royal Naval College at Dartmouth at the age of eighteen with the school report: "Prince Philip is a born leader, but he will need the exacting demands of a great service to do justice to himself. His best is outstanding; his second best is not good enough."

Possibly they had played together as children and they certainly met at the Coronation in 1937, but it was at Dartmouth, where Prince Philip gained the King's Dirk as the best all-round cadet, that he and Princess Elizabeth, who was accompanying her father and mother on a royal visit of inspection, first consciously became acquainted. Thereafter they maintained a correspondence, and Prince Philip sometimes spent his wartime leaves at Windsor.

There is reason to believe that when Princess Elizabeth was included in the royal tour of South Africa in 1947, the King and Queen regarded the occasion not only as an opportunity for their daughter to gain further experience of the duties of the Crown, but also as a chance to test the true depth of her feelings for Philip Mountbatten. Those close to the Princess were never in doubt of the result, and their views were sustained. For all the crowded programme of new vistas and new experiences, the months of separation did not weaken, but confirmed and increased, her love.

From Buckingham Palace on July 9th, 1947, came at last the expected announcement: "It is with the greatest pleasure that The King and Queen announce the betrothal of their dearly beloved daughter The Princess Elizabeth to Lieutenant Philip Mountbatten, R.N., son of the late Prince Andrew of Greece and Princess Andrew (Princess Alice of Battenberg), to which union The King has gladly given his consent."

Critics, of course, there had to be. Was such a high-spirited, polo-playing young man, who liked living hard and playing hard, driving at high speed and taking a home-made boat out in all weathers on somewhat precarious trips round the Orkneys, quite a suitable husband for the heiress presumptive? Admirable as such qualities of dash and daring might be in the Navy, in which he had gained promotion to the appointment of first lieutenant in H.M.S. *Wallace* at the age of twenty-one, surely someone more settled and serious would have been a better choice for consort of our future queen? Someone, perhaps, in keeping with Baron Stockmar's ideas on a husband for Queen Victoria: a man with "that earnest frame of mind which is ready of its own accord to sacrifice mere pleasure to real usefulness," and who would from the very outset accept his marriage as "a vocation of grave responsibility."

Beneath Philip's gaiety and free-and-easy manner, however, lay an unsuspected side of serious, constructive thought that was soon revealed in his speeches, and it was known that while naturally he took expert advice on the subject matter, he refused to allow his speeches to be written for him. He had given the assurance that he would say nothing untoward, but beyond that he would not go. If he could not say what he thought in his own words, he would say nothing at all.

Of his speeches, it was his presidential address to the meeting of the British Association for the Advancement of Science that was in particular to confound his remaining critics and bring a fuller appreciation of the extent of the nation's gain in Princess Elizabeth's choice. The British Association had been addressed by Albert, the Prince Consort, in 1859, and by the Duke of Windsor, then Prince of Wales, in 1926. The Prince of Wales discussed the invitation with his father, King George V, who warned him against accepting it. "The audience," he is reported to have said, "will consist of the most brilliant and formidable collection of brains in the country. The only member of the family who ever felt equal to the task of addressing them was your great-grandfather the Prince Consort, and he was an intellectual. These people once asked me to address them. I refused."

The Prince of Wales went ahead with the task, although it is generally understood that he had considerable help with the preparation of his address. Philip, however, insisted as usual on

87

choosing his own subject—the history of scientific achievement over the past hundred years. From information and advice obtained from leading scientists he then prepared his own speech which he wrote in his cabin in H.M.S. *Magpie* in the Mediterranean.

He spoke frankly, as a layman applying the subject of science to everyday needs and conditions.

"The instrument of scientific knowledge in our hands," he said, "is growing more powerful every day. Indeed, it has reached a point when we can either set the world free from drudgery, fear, hunger, and pestilence, or obliterate life itself.

"The nation's wealth and prosperity are governed by the rapid application of science to its industries and commerce. The nation's workers depend upon science for the maintenance and improvement of their standard of health, housing, and food.

"It is clearly our duty as citizens to see that science is used for the benefit of mankind. For of what use is science if man does not survive?"

It was not only his speech and capability that impressed, but also the way in which the royal president mixed with his erudite audience and showed his eagerness to learn from them.

On the eve of the wedding, Lieutenant Philip Mountbatten had a private audience at Buckingham Palace with the King. As Philip knelt before his future father-in-law, King George VI touched him on each shoulder with his sword in the ceremonial accolade, and then invested him with the insignia of a Knight Companion of the Most Noble Order of the Garter, the order to which he had but a few days before admitted his daughter, Princess Elizabeth. When Lieutenant Mountbatten rose from his knees, he was no longer a commoner but a royal duke.

"His Majesty has been pleased to authorise the use of the prefix, His Royal Highness, by Lieutenant Mountbatten," said the statement issued from Buckingham Palace, "and to approve that the dignity of a dukedom of the United Kingdom be conferred upon him by the name, style, and title of the Baron Greenwich of Greenwich in the County of London, Earl of Merioneth, and Duke of Edinburgh."

By these three titles the husband of the future Queen was united to each of the countries of Great Britain. The Dukedom of Edinburgh, previously held by Prince Alfred, the second son of Queen Victoria, had originally been bestowed in 1726 upon Frederick Lewis, eldest son of the Prince of Wales (afterwards George II).

The creation of the ancient earldom of Merioneth goes back into the mists of Welsh history. The title was held by one of the princes of Llewellyn the Great, who led the struggle for a Welsh revival early in the thirteenth century against the feudal Lords Marchers and their private armies.

The barony of Greenwich had been extinct since the death in 1794 of John Campbell, the second Duke of Argyll, who had received the honour in recognition of his services in Scotland in checking the Jacobite revolt against the accession of George I. Military leader though the previous holder of the barony had been, it is the Royal Navy with which Greenwich, home of the Royal Naval College and the National Maritime Museum, has so long been automatically associated. It was no doubt the desire to pay tribute to the naval service of the Duke as well as to represent the capital of the United Kingdom in his dignity that influenced the choice of this title.

Under his royal prerogative as the "Fountain of Honours," King George VI had bestowed the rank of H.R.H. upon his son-in-law, but when his grandmother, Queen Victoria, had wished to act similarly with regard to the husband of her youngest daughter, she had been frustrated. By a provision in the Treaty of the Congress of Vienna in 1815, each signatory agreed not to create titles of Royal Highness without the consent of the countries concerned. When Princess Beatrice married Prince Henry of Battenberg, who was not in his own right a royal prince, Queen Victoria wished to elevate him to the dignity of H.R.H., but the Kaiser objected and cited the Treaty of Vienna. As a result, Prince Henry was known as Serene Highness, the same title that was accorded to Queen Mary's brother, Prince Alexander of Teck, before he became Earl of Athlone.

Though regard to this clause in the Treaty seems to have been paid for a hundred years up to the outbreak of the First World War, the shattering upheavals of the twentieth century, with the rise and fall of monarchies and states, have left neither purpose nor desirability in the continued observance of the provision. The intriguing thought occurs that otherwise, not only republics but Soviet Russia as well would have had to sanction the creation of the Duke of Edinburgh's royal designation.

Part III

MANTLE OF MONARCHY

Baron

The wedding portrait

Topical Press

On the balcony at Buckingham Palace

Daily Graphic Picture Service

Returning from the Abbey

10

ROYAL WEDDING

THE year 1947 had been a black one in British history. The early months had seen the worst blizzards, the worst floods, and the severest winter of the century. Britain's newly nationalised coal industry had collapsed under the strain, causing a wholesale switch-off of power and a government-ordered shut-down of industry that for three weeks brought the country to a standstill on a scale not even approached by the General Strike of 1926. Where Hitler and his Luftwaffe had failed to paralyse industry, to silence the B.B.C., to stop publication of national periodicals, the coal crisis of 1947 succeeded. Firms that prided themselves on having maintained an unbroken record of production or service despite strikes, plagues, wars, and even the blitzing of office and factory, were suddenly faced with the fact that to attempt to continue that record would be an illegal act. In an ice-bound Britain it became an offence for a woman to warm her child at an electric fire.

For the year 1947 the coal crisis was not sufficient, however. The bulk of the American loan of over one thousand million pounds sterling, granted the previous year with the intention of setting a war-shattered Britain on her feet, had disappeared in almost as few months as it had been intended to last for years, and there was little to show for it but debt. Food imports were slashed; potatoes went on the ration. Two years after victory a shabby, badly-clothed, ill-housed Britain was tightening her belt to an extent that had not been known even in the worst years of the war.

Abroad, our fortunes seemed no happier. The term Empire had acquired a sudden opprobrium, and India's movement towards an independent republicanism had been feared by many to be the first step of a general dissolution. India made it plain, however, that although she desired a republican status she had no wish to leave the Commonwealth, and it was the late King George VI who did much behind the scenes to reconcile these wishes of the Indian Government. Even though her great-great-grandmother's proud title, "Empress of India," would no longer be inherited by that royal bride of November 20th, 1947, the Indian people were willing to recognise her as Head of the Commonwealth of which they remained members.

The day was grey as the fortunes of the year as Princess Elizabeth drove with her father in the Irish State Coach to Westminster. There had been suggestions that it would be more in keeping with Britain's grim realisation of austerity for the Princess to be married very quietly in St. George's Chapel, Windsor, scene of the wedding of King Edward VII. The House of Hanover generally had looked upon marriages within their family as personal occasions to be celebrated within the privacy of the royal chapels. Both King George V and Queen Victoria had been married in the Chapel Royal at St. James's Palace.

The wedding of King George VI, then Duke of York, and the Lady Elizabeth Bowes-Lyon in Westminster Abbey in 1923 was a departure from custom that created a precedent, but could hardly be regarded as having yet established a tradition that compelled observance.

The people, however, rose emphatically against such Jeremiahs and their advocacies of harsh economy and stringency.

In his tribute to the occasion John Masefield, the Poet Laureate, referred to the Crown as "a gleam, a star, to point men from despair," and it was as a gleam of hope and pride that the nation gladly seized the opportunity to celebrate the royal wedding in all its richness of pomp and dignity, and forget for a moment the drabness and depression of life amidst crises.

Seconding the faithful Commons' address of congratulation, Mr. Churchill, on behalf of the Opposition, summed up:

"There is no doubt that the approaching marriage gives keen and widespread pleasure in British homes, and that it stirs most warm and lively sympathies in the hearts of the British nation. Our constitutional monarchy and the Royal Family play a vital part in the tradition, dignity, and romance of our island life."

Quoting Shakespeare's "one touch of nature makes the whole world kin," he added: "Millions will welcome this joyous event as a flash of colour on the hard road we have to travel."

Even the Labour Member for the Shettleston Division of Glasgow, Mr. McGovern, a man well-known for his extreme socialist and republican views, was moved to remark that he had recently returned from Spain where they were hoping to get a constitutional monarchy of the type we had in this country. "The more I look at the red royal family in Moscow," he said, "the more I think the British Royal Family has a place still in the hearts of the people."

The world loves a wedding, and the world went to the wedding, with republican countries as keenly interested and enthusiastic as the world's few remaining kingdoms. To the *Sunday Times* a party of American journalists explained the interest of their own nation thus:

"This wedding is front-page news for us. You see, back home we feel the whole world is being turned upside-down, and we don't know where we are going. Out of the muddle, your Royal Family stands out for us as representing something really worth while as a symbol of decency and dignity and loyalty. So our readers want to know everything we can tell them about the wedding and about Britain."

In a dress designed from a painting by Botticelli, and embroidered with white Roses of York, with orange blossoms, and ears of corn and wheat, emblems of harvest and fertility, and with a train spun from silkworms at Lullingstone Castle, Princess Elizabeth drove with her father in the Irish State Coach to Westminster Abbey. The morning was still overcast, but there was sunlight in the pealing of the bells and the cheering and laughter of the crowds. The slow, emphatic strains of the National Anthem greeted the arrival of the coach at the West Door.

In my broadcast commentary upon the scene I recorded: "The doors of the coach are open. The crowd shouts with excitement and love. The King, in the uniform of Admiral of the Fleet, comes forward to help his daughter alight carefully. Now she steps down. A great cheer rises to sustain her.

"She pauses for a moment and looks at the Abbey. And perhaps—perhaps she is a little nervous in her heart as she passes from the grey of the morning outside into the warmth and colour of the Abbey."

The Princess walked with her father into the presence of history. With the greatness of the past—the bygone kings and queens, the statesmen, the poets, the soldiers; the Unknown Warrior brought from France to lie amongst the most illustrious in the land, symbol of heroism and the supreme sacrifice

"for God, for King and country, for loved ones, home and Empire, for the sacred cause of justice and the freedom of the world"—with this greatness of the past as silent witness, Elizabeth, the woman, took Philip, the man.

"Notwithstanding the splendour and national significance of the service in this Abbey," said Dr. Garbett, the Archbishop of York, in his address, "it is in all essentials exactly the same as it would be for any cottager who might be married this afternoon in some small country church in a remote village in the Dales. The same vows are taken; the same prayers are offered; the same blessings are given."

The essentials were the same. It was, like all weddings, a family wedding, a wedding in which the whole family of the British Commonwealth of Nations was able to share personally because of King George VI's permission that the royal wedding ceremony should be broadcast. In fact, by that miracle of radio the distant branches of the family in Canada and Australia were able to hear Princess Elizabeth's softly whispered response, "I will," which escaped all but those nearest the high altar and the shrine of St. Edward the Confessor in the Abbey itself.

So came to an end the simple service, for all the historic pageant and the magnificence of the setting, that is the fundamental symbol of life itself—the marrying and giving in marriage for the perpetuity of the human race, for the birth of new generations to take over the burdens of the old and to advance civilisation yet another step along the endless road of evolution. And the new was linked with the old, the past with the future, as a queen-to-be dropped in a curtsy and her consort bowed, rendering tribute both to King George and to Queen Mary as the symbol of the past from whose wisdom and experience the future would be developed. Thus, too, in an age when notions of chivalry and respect for elders have been sadly up-ended, did daughter and granddaughter give an inspiring lead in the practice of the fifth Commandment.

Hand in hand the royal couple proceeded slowly down the aisle and emerged from the Abbey to receive the full impact of crowds and noise surging up into a crescendo of cheers as first the bride with her long, lovely train, and then the bridegroom stepped into the coach. The horses pranced, the escort of Household Cavalry held itself ready. Then the signal was given, and to the rhythmic accompaniment of clattering hooves the regal glass coach bore the newly-married couple through the crowded streets to Buckingham Palace; to the wedding breakfast at which the King proposed their health—by tradition the sole toast on such an occasion; to crowds to be greeted from the balcony; to more crowds as, with the King and Queen leading the pursuit across the courtyard to shower them with rose petals, they drove away in an open landau drawn by four grey horses on the first stage of their honeymoon journey. Still the crowds followed them, dogging their first few days at Lord Mountbatten's Hampshire home, Broadlands. Not until they reached the rugged solitude of Birkhall in Scotland did they escape at last to the peace and privacy in which to enjoy those all-too-short honeymoon days.

In February 1948 Princess Elizabeth returned to the daily spotlight of her royal duties, a Princess confident and strengthened in the knowledge that she faced her future destiny with the support and comfort of the man she loved.

Meanwhile, the Duke of Edinburgh had returned to the Navy, not yet awhile to the sea that he loved, but attached temporarily to the Admiralty and to Greenwich.

On the occasion when Princess Elizabeth had launched the

34,000-ton liner, *Caronia*, she had been accompanied by Philip.

"I am so happy," Princess Elizabeth had said, "that on this, my third visit to Clydeside, my future husband is by my side."

Now, as her husband, he was to appear regularly at her side on tours that were not only extending the heiress presumptive's own knowledge of her future domain but training her consort for the role to which love had brought him.

He was with her when she paid her first visit to foreign soil in May 1948, and shared her first practical experience of the international aspect of the Crown. Fittingly, her father had chosen as her first training in this respect Paris, capital of the country which little more than a century before had been our traditional enemy and was now our main partner in maintaining democracy in Europe.

"The contrast between our ancient rivalries and the confidence which our two peoples feel in each other today is a striking one. It proves that among nations, as among individuals, the bitterest enmity can give way to friendship just as profound," Princess Elizabeth told the French.

"If we are to escape destruction, we must work for the breakdown of prejudices born of narrow-minded nationalism. All men who wish to preserve the values for which you and we have fought two wars side by side must look well beyond their frontiers. No country is morally self-sufficient, any more than it is economically self-supporting. Therefore we must be ready to throw into a common pool the gifts and virtues which are our most cherished heritage."

To the Duke of Edinburgh, who as a boy and prince of Greece at Gordonstoun had been apt to decry "all this royalty nonsense," came the appreciation of the fact that this official

99

visit to France was very different from others he had made before. The significance of their enthusiastic reception by the crowd was far more than a cordial welcome for a charming young couple.

"Part of that welcome may have been for us personally," commented the Duke afterwards. "At any rate, we liked to think so. But we are both convinced that the crowds who greeted us were expressing through us their friendship for our countrymen. Those waves and cheers were the spontaneous expression of the goodwill felt by the people of France for the people of this country, and if through us they have been able to see you, we are well satisfied."

In the Navy the Duke had learnt that a captain stands not only for himself but for his ship, the whole ship's company. Though the efficiency of the ship derives directly from the captain's personality and leadership, he cannot stand alone except in responsibility. Honours that may come to him are an acknowledgement not only of himself but of his ship.

The eminence brought to Philip by his marriage was a demonstration of this same naval doctrine, although on a much vaster scale. His acceptance and understanding of this tenet he made clear on June 8th, 1948, when after the Chamberlain's clerk had declared that the Duke of Edinburgh was "a man of good name and fame, and that he does not desire the freedom of this City whereby to defraud the King or this City or any of their rights, customs, or advantages, but that he will pay his scot, and bear his lot, and so they all say," he was made a Freeman of the City of London.

"Since the last war you have taken the opportunity of honouring those men who were principally responsible for the allied victory, all of them great leaders of men, whether in parliament or in civil life or on the field of battle," the Duke replied in acknowledging the honour. "But in every kind of human activity there are those who lead and those who follow. You have honoured the leaders. Now, if you will allow me, I would like to accept the Freedom of this City not only for myself but for all those millions who followed during the second World War. Our only distinction is that we did what we were told to do to the very best of our ability, and kept on doing it.

"The Chamberlain referred just now in rather flattering terms to my war record. The point I want to emphasise is something you all know. I would like to emphasise that there are hundreds upon thousands like it, and taken together they represent the endeavours of the followers during the last Great War, and so the greater part of our war effort. Good leaders undoubtedly got the best out of us, and without their leadership our efforts would have been fruitless. However, those leaders will not always be with us and the time will come when members of our generation will have to take their place. In peace, as in war, the followers have a great contribution to make to their country and to the cause of peace in the world generally."

Princess Elizabeth had broadcast her own dedication of service from South Africa on her twenty-first birthday. The Duke ended his speech by confirming his own assumption of a share in that testament.

"The ideal that my wife and I have set before us is to make the utmost use of the special opportunities we have to try to bring home to our own generation the full importance of that contribution and of the effort, both at work and at play, that is required of us."

II

PRINCE CHARLES

A YEAR less six days after the royal wedding, Buckingham
Palace issued an announcement, shortly after 10 p.m. on
November 14th, 1948:

"Her Royal Highness the Princess Elizabeth, Duchess of
Edinburgh, was safely delivered of a Prince at 9.14 p.m. today.
Her Royal Highness and her son are both doing well."

For the first time since the birth fifty-four years earlier of the
Duke of Windsor, a child had been born in direct line of
succession to the throne. The booming of the forty-one guns
—once the only means of notifying such news to the populace
with immediate dispatch—that signalled the birth of the royal
infant occasioned none of the novelty or surprise that had
accompanied the arrival into the world of his ancestors. A
narrow-minded Victorian dogma classed the subject of birth as
unmentionable, and any reference to, or even cognisance of,
pregnancy was regarded as being in the worst possible taste.
Such was the lack of preparedness and refusal to take notice of
Queen Alexandra's condition, in fact, that she was skating in
Windsor Park when she suddenly collapsed, and with no time
to await the arrival of the royal physicians, a local general
practitioner was summoned to assist at the premature birth of
Edward VII's first son, the Duke of Clarence. On the day that
her second son was born Queen Alexandra had been to an afternoon concert and had invited guests to dinner; the dinner-

party, however, had to proceed without its hostess, for that evening the future King George V arrived.

Even in the recent case of Prince Charles's grandmother, the world remained in complete ignorance until after the birth of Princess Elizabeth had occurred. Conforming to the old school of thought, King George V had forbidden the advance intimation that her father and mother, then Duke and Duchess of York, had wished to make.

For five months, however, since the publication of the statement that Princess Elizabeth would undertake no public engagements after the end of June, the nation had looked forward with the same family interest that had followed the wedding, to the arrival of a child who would provide yet another link of continuity in an hereditary monarchy that would remain steadfast and constant amidst all the change and turbulence of the twentieth century.

The immediate advent of the birth was heralded by a decision taken by King George VI by Letters Patent under the Great Seal of the Realm to fix the style and title of the children of the marriage between Princess Elizabeth and the Duke of Edinburgh.

"It is declared by the Letters Patent," announced the *London Gazette* of November 9th, 1948, "that the children of the aforesaid marriage shall have, and at all time hold and enjoy the style, title, or attribute of Royal Highness and the titular dignity of Prince or Princess prefixed to their respective Christian names in addition to any other appellations and titles of honour which may belong to them thereafter."

By taking this step the King amended the proclamation made by his father, George V, in 1917, which limited the style of H.R.H. to children of the sovereign and children of the

sons of the sovereign, and excluded the children of the daughters of the sovereign. The effect of this proclamation has been
seen in the case of the two sons of the Princess Royal, the Earl
of Harewood and the Hon. Gerald Lascelles, who bear no
royal titles. By this limitation, also, neither the children of
Prince William nor Prince Richard of Gloucester, nor those of
the Duke of Kent and his sister and brother, Princess Alexandra
and Prince Michael, will succeed to any royal designation as
prince or princess.

King George VI's amendment of his father's edict does not
affect Princess Margaret, whose children will inherit no royal
title, but applied only to Princess Elizabeth. Had the King not
taken this step, Princess Elizabeth's son, in accordance with
normal practice in the ordinary peerage, would have been accorded his father's second title, Earl of Merioneth. This custom
is followed also by royal houses in other countries, although
our own royal family make a distinction where a dukedom of
the Blood Royal is involved. The son is then known by his
father's family name, as in the case of Prince William of
Gloucester, and Prince Michael of Kent. So far as Princess
Elizabeth's daughter is concerned, she would have been known
as Lady Anne Mountbatten, her father's adopted surname, but
for her grandfather's intervention.

Mountbatten would have been the name also of our next
royal house, of which upon his accession Prince Charles would
have been the first sovereign, had not the Queen on April 9th,
1952, declared "her will and pleasure that she and her children
shall be styled and known as the House and Family of Windsor,
and that their descendants, other than female descendants who
marry and their descendants, shall bear the name of Windsor."

As a result, Prince Charles will become instead the fifth

sovereign of the House of Windsor, the dynasty King George V founded in 1917, when as a consequence of the Great War he abandoned the German House name of Saxe-Coburg-Gotha that had descended to him through his father, Edward VII, from the Prince Consort. The ultimate accession of Prince Charles will also mean that for six successive generations the Crown has passed in an uninterrupted family descent, the first time that this has occurred since the days of the early Plantagenets. The succession then had been broken by the death in 1376—a year before that of his father—of the Black Prince, who instituted the three ostrich feathers and motto, "I Serve," as the crest of the Prince of Wales. In the following year, 1377, Edward III was succeeded by his grandson, Richard II.

Four generations of the House of Windsor gathered in the nursery at Buckingham Palace. In the babe in the cot, Prince Charles Philip Arthur George, second in succession to the throne of Great Britain, Northern Ireland and the British Dominions beyond the Seas, thirty-second descendant of William the Conqueror, were linked also the lineages of Mary, Queen of Scots, Robert the Bruce, James Stuart, who united the thrones of Scotland and England, the Electress Sophia.

For months, particularly anxious that Princess Elizabeth should have no worry to mar her approach to motherhood, King George VI had fought pain and striven to conceal his ill health. He held out to the end. As a father, he saw his daughter through the crowning achievement of a woman's life. As Sovereign, he had the satisfaction of knowing that with God's Grace the direct continuity of the Crown was established for at least two generations. He was content. His immediate objective accomplished, the reaction from the strain set in suddenly. He surrendered himself at last to his doctors.

In the same month that his grandson was born, George the Sixth became officially sick. He was suffering, his doctors diagnosed, from a severe physical affliction caused by an obstruction to circulation in the arteries of the leg. Prolonged treatment and complete rest were essential. He would be unable to make the tour of Australia and New Zealand that had been planned for the following spring.

THE MANTLE DONNED

"I SAID to the man who stood at the gate of the year, 'Give me a light that I may tread safely into the unknown,' " King George VI had quoted from a poem by Louise Haskins in one of his famous Christmas broadcasts. "And he replied, 'Go out into the darkness and put your hand into the hand of God. That shall be to you better than light, and safer than a known way.'"

From that first serious illness of 1948 George the Sixth must have realised that he stood at the gate of the unknown: he was a man, as Mr. Churchill said, who walked with death as his companion. For himself he had no concern. He had "put his hand into the hand of God" and, though he used John Bunyan's words, he spoke for himself when he declared at Christmas 1950, "Whatever comes or does not come, I will not be afraid."

Time was getting short. To the nation at large the King's health in those post-war years had become increasingly a matter of deep concern; how much graver the concern of those within the intimacy of the royal family circle, acquainted with the full facts about His Majesty's condition and the awareness that the sands of life were running out.

Princess Elizabeth did all that she could to ease the burden of monarchy from her father's shoulders and the King, though concerned lest she should overtax her strength as he had done his own, concentrated upon extending and intensifying the training of his daughter, so that when the day came for her to assume the Crown she would be as fully equipped for the task as was humanly possible.

Experience flooded upon experience. There was so much to be grasped, so much to be understood, so much of the country and of the Commonwealth to be visited, so many sections of the community to be met. Princess Elizabeth was learning rapidly, not only for herself but for all of her generation. Every new understanding and appreciation, every new experience, whether official or purely personal, she sought to pass on for the practical benefit of others in fulfilment of her pledge of service.

From her own experience of motherhood she strove to allay the worries of all those who might be facing the natural event of birth with fear and superstition. Professor R. W. Johnstone, the obstetrician, had held up Princess Elizabeth as an example. "I believe," he said, "that the simple and natural way in which she has accepted the dignity and responsibility of motherhood has been an inspiring model to the young womanhood of the whole of the English-speaking world."

But Princess Elizabeth was not content to lead by example alone. She wanted to take a more direct, vigorous course. She knew, as her own gynæcologist, Sir William Gilliatt, who attended at the birth of Prince Charles, had told her, that "healthy babies cannot be born but of healthy mothers." In the interests of the national family she wanted everyone to realise the fact and act upon it.

To the Royal College of Obstetricians and Gynæcologists she declared, upon admission to honorary fellowship: "Your work is a powerful force in creating in the minds of women a calm sense of confidence and security as the time of their baby's birth draws near. It is good that every woman should have this peace of mind at such a great and thrilling moment of her life." To the National Association for Maternity and Child Welfare she stressed the truth already apparent in the results of fifty years of maternity and child welfare that had reduced the mortality figures for babies in the first year of life from one hundred and fifty-four to under thirty out of every thousand.

"Mothers," said Princess Elizabeth, "are being shown the ancient truth that having children is a beautiful and natural event which need not be made dark and ugly by the shadow of fear."

With her parents, Princess Elizabeth had toured South Africa. Mainly she had been in the background, although she had named a new dock after herself and had borne the spotlight of her coming-of-age broadcast. She had travelled eight thousand miles, rushed here and there, ceaselessly on the move. She had discovered that, no matter how comfortable and luxurious the travel, fatigue was unavoidable with so much ground to be covered and so vast a programme to be compressed into so short a time. Though fatigue is the natural reaction of an overworked human body, it is not a state permissible in royalty. No matter how tired and exhausted, how wearied by the endless repetition of the same receptions, the same speeches, the same presentations of local civic dignitaries, there must always be the appearance of freshness and vitality, of lively interest and sincerity.

One remark by Princess Elizabeth to a South African official, that she felt guilty at enjoying herself when the people at home in an icebound Britain were suffering in the throes of a coal crisis, drew from the American news magazine *Time* the comment:

"It was a statement worthy of the future Queen, not only because it was gracious and considerate, but because the royal heiress, for all her pretty apology, wasn't really having much fun."

Unfortunately, there is still in this country a section of the community that considers no sovereign or future sovereign entitled to "have fun." One particular occasion in her married life that gave Princess Elizabeth the opportunity of true, natural happiness was when she went to join her husband as a naval officer's wife in Malta, and that was spoiled for her by ill-judged criticisms.

From the formality of his office as consort of the heiress presumptive, the Duke of Edinburgh had returned to active service with the Navy and had been appointed to the command of H.M.S. *Magpie*. He picked up readily the threads of his career in a typical speech that won the ship's company solidly to his support. He realised, the Duke told them genially, that it might prove a handicap and embarrassment to have him as their captain. Any man with black eyes who came up before him on a charge could therefore be sure that he would have the Duke on his side.

The problem of the serving officer's wife is a time-old one. She is ever torn between husband and children. Naturally it is the husband who bears the brunt of the separation. He can be joined by his wife only at certain times and at certain stations. It is true no doubt that arrangements could have been made for the Duke to relinquish active service and remain at home, but what wife, particularly the daughter of a naval officer, would wish to interfere with her husband's career?

Still foremost a naval officer, the Duke knew that his duty lay with the Fleet. It was apparent, too, that in keeping with his ultimate position as consort of the Queen he would be given eventually high naval rank. While the opportunity still existed, he wished to earn for himself as much as possible of the gold braid.

Malta is one of the naval stations offering facilities for wives and, in common with others, Princess Elizabeth took the opportunity of joining her husband. For once it seemed that she might escape from the studied formality that must ever be maintained at home to the natural joys of a young woman in her twenty-fifth year. Even so, she remembered the obligations of her birth to the extent of fulfilling some fifty official engagements on the George Cross island.

Unfortunately, to one newspaper to which little but circulation is sacred, the circumstances of that brief respite preceding a crowded Canadian tour—a mission which she accomplished in a manner that no one, Mr. Churchill declared, "has surpassed in brilliance and living force"—lent themselves to the provocation of an irresistible controversy. Without regard for the feelings of a young wife and mother upon whom, within a year, the full burden of sovereignty was to descend and to whom any further chance of a private holiday was to be denied, the newspaper began to carp, with the worst possible sensationalism, about the Princess's absence and alleged neglect of her children. Such nonsensical proportions did this stirred-up controversy reach that some who rushed chivalrously to the defence of the Princess sought experts' advice to make out a case that separation from its mother was beneficial to a child in that it developed self-reliance.

Whatever the criticism, whatever the attack, royalty can make no reply, offer no explanation. Only those close to the royal family circle knew how deeply Princess Elizabeth had been hurt and upset by the ill-judged censure. Once again it was made forcefully clear to her that royalty can never be off parade. There is no escape from the critical glare of constant scrutiny and investigation.

In a small way the sojourn of the royal ambassadress, with the official tours made by her and the Duke about the island— the reason that the Crown's advisers made no attempt to recall her from her husband—served as training for the first major tour that King George VI decided his daughter was now ready to undertake: the tour of Canada in the autumn of 1951.

When the time came, however, the departure of Princess Elizabeth and the Duke of Edinburgh was delayed by a recurrence of the King's ill health, which resulted in an operation on his lung on September the 23rd. Ultimately, in an attempt to catch up on an overcrowded programme, the royal couple left by air instead of sea. The operation had been successful and and King was recovering, but, even so, at such a time no daughter bound by strong ties of love and filial devotion would have chosen voluntarily to travel overseas. To the strain of the tour was therefore added this intimate anxiety which distance and separation helped only to increase. As heiress presumptive, Princess Elizabeth realised, however, that she could not allow her personal feelings to interfere with the opportunity to serve Britain and the Commonwealth in a manner not open to anyone else.

During the war the British premiership—with the vigorous personality of Winston Churchill and the freedom, of which he took full advantage, from the constitutional fetters surrounding the throne—did develop considerably into a practical rallying-point and focus of unity not only for the Empire but also for the Allied nations. With the end of the war and the resurgence of domestic rivalries, the office of prime minister became once more instinctively associated with a political

school of thought. No matter how striking the personality of the man in office, he would be welcomed in other countries of the Commonwealth, where views on government are divided by similar rival political factions, with an awareness of his political colouring and a partial distrust of the purpose of his visit. Even of men without political affiliation—expert economists, financiers, trade delegates—suspicion of concealed motive and underlying interests, and an instinctive guardedness would never be far away, particularly in these days of world shortages and stringency.

The throne, however, has no axes to grind. Free of political aura and financial interests, the Crown can inspire the nations of the Commonwealth into unified action; into making the most of their respective resources in the interests of all; into a revival of the realisation that, beyond the mercenary side of trade and exchange, which in the immediate urgency of post-war conditions have been apt to dominate the relationship, lies the true, deeper significance of spiritual brotherhood.

With this understanding of the task before her, Princess Elizabeth left her father's bedside to journey through ten of Canada's provinces. Though this was intended to be but the first of several visits, and not an attempt to tour Canada comprehensively, the extent of the tour and distances involved in the five weeks allotted, allowed but a fleeting glimpse of the heart of Canada. Each town, each city on the route meant the apparently unavoidable repetition of similar civic receptions, and endless presentations of the same class of dignitary and official. It was a monopoly of time by officialdom at the expense of the greater interest and value in meeting the ordinary people and acquiring a direct knowledge of their work and play, their way of life.

In England, Princess Elizabeth had sought to awaken people to a true understanding of the nation's various activities, their significance and the problems involved. To attempt to repeat this pattern in her speeches in Canada, she appreciated, would be a grave error. True, the Crown of which the heiress presumptive was a representative, was symbolically as much a part of Canada as it was of Britain. In her farewell broadcast to the people of the Dominion Princess Elizabeth drew attention to the fact.

"I am well aware," she said, "that the acclaim you have given us, which has often seemed to me to have the breadth and immensity of the sea, has had a far deeper meaning in it than a personal welcome, and this has often made me think of the words spoken by the Governor-General in Ottawa during the first day of our visit. He said then that the link with the Crown was a thing of real and tangible strength, and one of the most important factors in uniting the people of the Commonwealth into one great brotherhood. You have shown me the reality of this, and I thank you for it. Destiny has given me the great privilege of being able to live my life for the service of that brotherhood. In these five weeks you have given me a new strength and inspiration which I know will always help me in the future."

The position remained, however, that as a woman Princess Elizabeth was a stranger visiting the country for the first time. It was impossible, without an implication of presumption, for her to try to lead Canadians into an understanding of their own country and domestic problems. Wisely, therefore, she adopted throughout a theme of thanks for all that was being shown to her.

"We shall take with us memories that will always draw us

back to this country, the towering buildings of your big cities and the charm of your smaller communities; the blue skies and golden colours of autumn—'the fall,' as I have now learned to call it—and the trees and fields beneath the first snow of winter: all the beauty and the majesty of Canada. I thank you for having shown me these things, and I am grateful for a glimpse you have given me of the greatness of this nation and the even greater future which is within its grasp. I have seen this future in the eyes of hundreds and thousands of your children, and have heard it in their voices."

In a farewell speech at Halifax, the Duke of Edinburgh echoed his wife's words:

"We take back a fairly comprehensive picture of Canada. We have seen you at work and at play. We have seen your homes and your children and we have prayed with you in your churches. We have seen the forests and the wheatfields, factories and universities, scientists and armed services, and we have learnt something of your hopes and fears."

Possibly it is primarily upon the symbolism of the Crown that the success of any royal tour in any Commonwealth country depends, and by comparison the holder of the office, the individual, matters little. In Canada, however, on the first major tour abroad in which she was principal, it was Princess Elizabeth in herself who captured the hearts in a manner that went far beyond the requirements of formal sovereignty.

There is a general assumption that anyone in direct succession to the throne is automatically endowed with a strictly serious outlook and stiff, unbending dignity. Regal and dignified the Princess was by second nature, but she was also a young woman of grace and charm who could laugh with youthful gaiety when the royal train once inadvertently steamed away without her; who, in her enthusiasm for the literary treasures in the university library at New Brunswick, could spontaneously read aloud the lines from "Our Lady of the Snows" that Rudyard Kipling had penned on a map of Canada:

> "A nation spoke to a nation,
>   A queen sent word to a throne:
>   'Daughter am I in my mother's house,
>   But mistress in my own . . .' "

Some writers, making capital out of the economic situation and the currency differences which at the moment isolate Canada from the free intercourse of the Commonwealth's sterling group of nations, have tried to make out that Canada is moving away from Britain and closer to the United States. Whether or not there has ever been the slightest foundation for such a suggestion, Princess Elizabeth succeeded not only in inspiring a loyalty for the family tie that she personified, but in arousing for herself a love and affection of real and practical value for the future.

Certainly on that brief visit to the United States before her return to Britain it was personality alone that won the day. Among countries following a democratic way of life the United States is at the far end of the scale from any form of monarchy, but in that country where monarchy is an institution often violently distrusted, Princess Elizabeth and her consort drew cheers of approval, even from those who had come to scoff.

The Times Washington correspondent recorded the following comment by one American reporter at the end of the royal Press reception:

Baron

With Prince Charles in the Spring of 1949

Princess Margaret

Baron

"You heard no mutterings from cynics, chauvinists, professional proletarians. Royalty would not fit into this country's scheme of things, but how glad we are for the British, with whom we are destined to stand shoulder to shoulder in the uncertain world ahead, that they have a Princess who is so capably being the symbol of British lustre, dignity, and strength."

And the President of the United States was moved to proclaim: "We have had many distinguished visitors here in this city, but never before have we had such a wonderful young couple that so completely captured the hearts of us all."

In his address Mr. Truman continued: "This country is built upon principles that we have inherited from the British people—our love of liberty, our system of justice, which is based upon the English Common Law, our language—these and many other things have given us a strong feeling of kinship.

"Over the years we have built these ties into a remarkable international friendship. We have had our differences in the past, but today it would be just as hard to imagine a war between our countries as it would be to imagine another war between the states of this country. It just could not happen.

"I hope the day will come soon when the same thing will be true among all nations of the world—when war will be impossible in the world. That depends in great measure upon how well our two countries stick together and work for world peace. I am sure we will do a better job for world peace because your visit has tightened the bonds between us."

From Canada, Princess Elizabeth returned with "a new sense of faith in the progress of mankind."

"For none of the doubts, disillusions, nor difficulties that face us on this troubled continent are going to hold back the Canadians," she said. "They are going to ensure for themselves the survival of all those things for which we have fought in this country through the ages, and which we treasure—justice, liberty, opportunity for all, and kindliness between man and man. And by so doing they are going to ensure this for others, too."

At the Guildhall, in London, the Prime Minister welcomed back the heiress presumptive with the nation's thanks to her "for what you have done for us, and to Providence for having endowed you with the gifts and personality which are not only precious to the British Commonwealth and Empire and its islands at home, but will play their part in assuring and mellowing the forward march of human society all the world over.

"The symbol of the Crown and the preservation throughout the centuries of the British monarchy," added Mr. Churchill, "have rendered possible a sense of unity of which time and space, which so often divided, have become the servants and ceased to be the masters. And all this evolution would not survive the changes of the modern world if it were not sustained and refreshed by the personal contribution made in recent generations by the occupants of, and heirs to, the throne."

At Sandringham the King's mother, Queen Mary, his wife, daughters and grandchildren, his brother and sisters-in-law, his nephews and nieces of Kent and Gloucester, gathered with him about the family fireside to make Christmas 1951 one of the most complete and memorable occasions. Though he was still convalescent and his doctors were anxious that he should be spared even the slightest strain, George the Sixth, in the intimacy of his own private circle, could not forget, at that greatest of family festivals, the wider family of which he was head: the peoples of whom he thought as "one great family, for that is how we are learning to live. We all belong to each other. We all need each other. It is in serving each other and in sacrificing for our common good that we are finding our true life."

Where the blast of war had failed to interrupt his Christmas broadcasts, the King was determined that no frailty of the flesh should succeed. He made up his mind that through radio he would join his peoples as usual at their own celebrations in their own homes to give them his personal greetings. Finally, he met his doctors to the extent of agreeing to record his message beforehand so that the strain on his voice and strength might be eased as much as possible.

Courage, however, could not hide the betrayal of his voice that he was still a sick man as he thanked his doctors and nurses for their care and devotion, and his peoples for their solicitude over his health. He spoke of friendliness and kindness; of how precious this spirit was in an age often hard and cruel, and needing the "example of tolerance and understanding that runs like a golden thread through the great and diverse family of the British Commonwealth of Nations."

"I think," said King George VI in his last message to his peoples, "that among all the blessings which we may count today, the chief one is that we are a friendly people."

Once again his tour of Australia and New Zealand, which had had to be cancelled in 1949 and had been planned afresh for 1952, was out of question. The doctors advised that he must continue a prolonged convalescence until he had sufficiently recovered his strength to reap the full benefit of a sea cruise in H.M.S. *Vanguard*.

Instead, therefore, Princess Elizabeth, with the Duke of Edinburgh, undertook the tour in the place of her father. From London Airport on a bitter wintry day the King waved farewell to his daughter as she left by air for a short official visit in Kenya that would refresh her for the main tour ahead. Standing within six feet of His Majesty, I remember the long, searching look which he gave his daughter as she turned to wave for the last time from the door of the aircraft. He was never to see her again.

George the Sixth returned to Sandringham, where he was as free as he ever could be from the trappings of monarchy and state; where the villagers neither stared nor intruded, but accepted him naturally as their squire.

That week-end the weather was still cold, but fine. By the frozen lake the King watched his grandson, Prince Charles, playing.

On Tuesday, February 5th, 1952, free from pain and in good spirits, the King went shooting. After a quiet family dinner-party he took a last walk round the grounds of the house where he was born, the home that he loved best of all; the grounds to which his mother, Queen Mary, had devoted such a labour of love in their replanning and creation into a scene of joy and beauty. As he walked in the still calm of the winter evening he was already looking forward to a shoot the following day if the weather held.

The King was surely a man content and at peace. There is no stage at which training for sovereignty can be said to end, but the manner in which his daughter had fulfilled her first major role in that mission to Canada must have exceeded even a proud father's expectations, and given him the assurance that when the time came for her to wear the Crown she would not falter. He had seen her happily married and knew that she would have the love and support of her devoted husband and family to help her to bear the burden. He had seen, too, the affection and esteem that she had earned in the hearts of the people.

The world was still troubled and chaotic, but the elections of three months before had done something to stabilise home affairs after the uncertainty of those months of government by a party with the most precarious of majorities. Though the King himself was above political partisanship, he would naturally have desired that when the time came for his daughter to begin her reign she should have the assistance of a strong and stable government, whatever its political colouring. As it was, he could have found to guide her first steps on the lonely path of constitutional monarchy no better statesman than that brilliant and robust campaigner, Winston Churchill, with his vast fund of experience both as politician and historian.

George the Sixth, by the Grace of God, of Great Britain, Northern Ireland, and the British Dominions beyond the Seas, King, Defender of the Faith, retired peacefully to his room and fell asleep for the last time.

In Kenya, his twenty-five-years-old daughter was making her way along a jungle path to a "hide" from which she could watch the big game. Suddenly from out of the shadows an elephant emerged and stood in her path. Without flinching, Princess Elizabeth continued to walk steadily towards the elephant until she had reached the "hide." Quietly she climbed the ladder to the platform in the treetops.

"Ma'am," said Mr. Sherborne Walker, the owner of the Treetops Hotel, "if you have the same courage in facing whatever the future sends you, as you have in facing an elephant at ten yards, we are going to be very fortunate."

THE ACCESSION

KENSINGTON PALACE. June 20th, 1837.

  "I was awoke at 6 o'clock by Mamma, who told me that the Archbishop of Canterbury and Lord Conyngham were here and wished to see me. I got out of bed and went into my sitting-room (only in my dressing-gown) and *alone*, and saw them. Lord Conyngham then acquainted me that my poor uncle, the King, was no more, and consequently that I am *Queen*."

It was nearly 115 years since Queen Victoria, then a slender, fair-haired girl of eighteen, with a small chin and prominent blue eyes, recorded that entry in her diary: nearly 115 years since a woman had succeeded to the throne of Britain, although her reign, which had been ended only a matter of fifty-one years, was still within living memory.

The fact that the new Queen Elizabeth was abroad at the time of her accession created no new precedent or problems. Edward I was proclaimed king during his absence in Palestine on the Crusades, and his coronation did not take place until two years afterwards. The last sovereign to succeed to the throne whilst abroad was George I, son of the Electress Sophia of Hanover. By a matter of weeks Queen Anne had outlived the Electress, who had been named as heiress under the Act of Settlement, and who had so much coveted the Crown. By that same Act, therefore, the Crown passed to her son. His absence from the country was due primarily to Anne herself who, having in her youth been jilted before the Court by Prince George of Hanover, had no love for the family and had furiously resisted all suggestions that the Electress and her son should be invited to take up residence in England. There can be no doubt that Anne clung to the hope that so long as the Hanovers remained out of England there was a chance that her stepbrother, James Stuart, whom she and her sister Mary had virtually robbed of his birthright, might renounce his Roman Catholic faith and enable her to fight for his succession instead.

George I did not arrive in England until nearly two months after Anne's death. In 1952, Queen Elizabeth spanned half the world by air to reach the capital of her realm in less than twenty hours.

Whilst the Queen was still embarking upon the first stage of her four-thousand-miles flight home, the Accession Council met at the Ambassador's Court of St. James's Palace for the formal proclamation of her accession, and Members of Parliament and peers began to take the Oath of Allegiance to their new sovereign.

The Accession Council is a much older body than the Privy Council, which was originally an assembly entrusted with the king's secret business. Older than the House of Lords and going back beyond the Great Council of the Realm, the council of mediæval kings, the Accession Council probably has its origin in the Anglo-Saxon Witenagemot, the assembly which met to choose and proclaim a new sovereign. Numbering over three hundred members, the Accession Council includes, in addition to the members of the late sovereign's Privy Council, the "Lords Spiritual and Temporal of this realm" and "numbers of other principal gentlemen of quality, with the Lord Mayor, Aldermen, and Citizens of London."

The proclamation was, of course, no more than a traditional formality, as was the subsequent Accession Declaration to uphold the Protestant Succession to the Throne and to maintain the security of the Established Church of Scotland. The heiress presumptive had automatically become Queen the instant her father died, and her accession was in no way dependent upon these ceremonies.

Up to the thirteenth century there was invariably an interregnum, a period between the death of one king and the crowning of his successor, when the country was without sovereign or formal rule. Justice has always been—and still is—a part of the royal prerogative, which meant that whilst there was no sovereign there was also no "Fountain of Justice." The King's Peace temporarily ceased to exist and crime could be committed with impunity and without legal redress.

"There was tribulation soon in the land, for every man that could forthwith robbed another," recorded an observer at the time of the death of Henry I.

When Henry III died the absence of his heir, Edward I, with the Crusades meant a prolonged interregnum before he could return to be crowned, and this would have resulted in an impossible situation. The King's Peace was therefore sworn forthwith, and on the day that his father was buried it was proclaimed that the reign of Edward I had begun. By the time of Edward IV the rule was established that upon the demise of a sovereign no interregnum, or break in formal rule, occurred. The Crown thus acquired a dual conception. It became an immortal symbol of power and authority that continued without regard for the demise of the sovereign's human body, and as such passed automatically without interruption to the heir. In 1608 it was legally upheld that by the laws of England there

Watching a procession from the wall of Clarence House, November 1950

Karsh

A portrait taken for the 1951 Canadian Tour

was no such thing as a state of interregnum and that "coronation is but a royal ornament and solemnisation of the royal descent, but no part of the title."

Even when the principle that the king does not die was firmly accepted, the perpetuity of the Crown did not at first apply to its servants. These were considered to be the personal officers of the dead sovereign, and parliament also was regarded as owing its existence personally to the sovereign who had summoned it in the first instance. With the death of the sovereign, therefore, parliament was automatically dissolved and officials holding Crown appointments had to vacate them.

The reign of Anne brought matters to a head. With her persistent refusal to invite the named heiress presumptive, the Electress Sophia of Hanover, to England, it was obvious that upon Anne's death there would be some considerable delay before the new sovereign could arrive in the country. With no Privy Council or Crown officials in existence the field would be left wide open for Jacobite sympathisers to stake the claims of James Stuart. To thwart any such action the Succession to the Crown Act was passed in 1707. This continued the life of the Privy Council and the duration of Crown appointments for a period of six months after the demise of the sovereign.

In Queen Victoria's reign the validity of military commissions was removed from all contingency upon the sovereign's life; and finally the holding of all offices under the Crown was declared unaffected by the Demise of the Crown Act, 1910.

Meanwhile the Representation of the People Act in 1867, the climax of a series of statutes which had spread over the years from 1696, finally established the existence of parliament as a separate entity unaffected by the sovereign's demise.

Thus, whilst Queen Elizabeth the Second was still on her

way back to England, Parliament, Privy Council, Justice and all Crown appointments continued uninterrupted without the necessity for any action on her part. His Majesty's Forces had immediately become Her Majesty's Forces; King's Counsel had automatically changed to Queen's Counsel.

One issue that Queen Elizabeth's accession settled for all time was the question of coparcenary in relation to the throne. Under feudal law, since her father had died without a male heir, both she and her sister, Princess Margaret, would have shared as joint heirs in his estate, and questions on this principle were in fact raised in the House of Commons in 1937. At the time the Home Secretary, Sir John Simon, replied that there was no doubt in the circumstances that Her Royal Highness Princess Elizabeth would succeed as sole heir. Now she had done so.

On February 8th, 1952, Queen Elizabeth convened the first meeting of her Privy Council at St. James's Palace.

"By the sudden death of my dear father I am called to assume the duties and responsibility of sovereignty," she said in her Accession Speech to the Council.

"At this time of deep sorrow it is a profound consolation to me to be assured of the sympathy which you and all my peoples feel toward me, to my mother and my sister, and to the other members of my family. My father was our revered and beloved head, as he was of the wider family of his subjects. The grief which his loss brings is shared among us all.

"My heart is too full for me to say more to you today than that I shall always work, as my father did throughout his reign, to uphold constitutional government and to advance the happiness and prosperity of my peoples, spread as they are all the world over. I know that in my resolve to follow his shining example of service and devotion I shall be inspired by the loyalty and affection of those whose Queen I have been called to be, and by the counsel of their elected parliaments.

"I pray that God will help me to discharge worthily this heavy task that has been laid upon me so early in my life."

Shortly afterwards, at 11 a.m., resplendent in cockaded hats and brilliant, gold-emblazoned tabards, the Kings-of-Arms, the Heralds and the Pursuivants gathered on the balcony at St. James' Palace overlooking the crowded Friary Court. Preceded by a fanfare from the State trumpeters, Sir George Bellew, Garter King of Arms, unrolled a scroll of parchment and read the first of the series of public proclamations that would echo throughout the cities of Great Britain, Northern Ireland, and the Commonwealth:

"Whereas it hath pleased Almighty God to call to His mercy our late Sovereign Lord King George the Sixth of blessed and glorious memory, by whose decease the Crown is solely and rightfully come to the High and Mighty Princess Elizabeth Alexandra Mary, we therefore Lords spiritual and temporal of this Realm being assisted with these of his late Majesty's Privy Counsellors with representatives of other members of the Commonwealth with other principal gentleman of quality with the Lord Mayor Aldermen and Citizens of London do now hereby with one voice and consent of tongue and heart publish and proclaim the High and Mighty Princess Elizabeth Alexandra Mary is now by death of our late Sovereign of happy memory become Queen Elizabeth the Second, by the Grace of God Queen of this Realm and all her other realms and territories head of the Commonwealth Defender of the Faith to whom her lieges do acknowledge all faith and constant obedience with hearty and humble affection; beseeching God by whom kings and queens do reign to bless the Royal Princess Elizabeth the Second with long and happy years to reign over us—

God Save The Queen."

Queen Elizabeth was the first sovereign to be proclaimed "Head of the Commonwealth," a title which was the consequence of India's decision to become a republic, although still remaining a member of the Commonwealth of Nations, and which replaced her great-great-grandmother's title of Empress of India.

There was another notable alteration of the terms in which her father's accession had been proclaimed. He had been described as: "of Great Britain, Ireland, and the British Dominions beyond the Seas." Queen Elizabeth was referred to as "Queen of this Realm and all her other realms and territories."

In the House of Commons Mr. Churchill gave the following explanation:

"The House will observe in the Royal Proclamation the importance and significance of the word 'realm.' There was a time, not so long ago, when the word 'dominion' was greatly esteemed, but now, almost instinctively and certainly spontaneously, the many nations and races have found in the word 'realm' an expression of their sense of unity, combined in most cases with positive allegiance to the Crown or proud and respectful association with it. Thus we go forward on our long and anxious journey, moving together in freedom and in hope, spread across the oceans and under every sky and climate though we be."

In front of the Paris Opera House

In the garden of Clarence House

Some responsible sources were inclined to draw a much broader inference from the changed description, however. Generally, it was believed that the change had resulted from representations from one or more of the Dominions. Canada, in particular, had on one or two occasions given evidence of a desire to change from the status of a self-governing Dominion to that of a sister Kingdom of Great Britain with the title, "Kingdom of Canada." Support for this belief was further forthcoming when Canada proclaimed Queen Elizabeth's accession with the words "our own lawful and rightful liege Lady Elizabeth II by the Grace of God, of Great Britain, Ireland, and the British Dominions beyond the Seas, Queen, Defender of the Faith, supreme Liege Lady in and over Canada." South Africa, using the same original description that had applied to her father, added the words "Supreme Sovereign in and over South Africa," while Australia followed the same form as Canada.

If this inference is correct and the trend materialises, it seems that within her reign Queen Elizabeth may find herself wearing not one crown but several; the link uniting the different countries of the Commonwealth may be no longer the acceptance of one indivisible Crown, but the person of the holder, in this case Queen Elizabeth herself.

The flags and standards that had temporarily soared to the mastheads for the proclamation of the accession of the Queen, returned to the half-mast position as the nation mourned the passing of a beloved sovereign.

From the small village church at Sandringham where he had been guarded by gamekeepers from his estate, the dead King was brought to Westminster Hall to lie-in-state, while night and day an endless train of his people filed past in silent homage. As I watched one night that moving panorama of tribute and love, I broadcast these impressions.

It is dark in New Palace Yard at Westminster tonight. As I look down from this old, leaded window I can see the ancient courtyard dappled with little pools of light where the lamps of London try to pierce the biting, wintry gloom —and fail. Moving through the darkness of the night is an even darker stream of human beings, coming, almost noiselessly, from under a long white canopy that crosses the pavement and ends at the great doors of Westminster Hall. They speak very little, these people, but their footsteps sound faintly as they cross the yard and go out through the gates, back into the night from which they came.

They are passing in their thousands through the hall of history while history is being made. No one knows from where they come or where they go, but they are the people, and to watch them pass is to see the nation pass.

It is very simple, this lying-in-state of a dead King, and of incomparable beauty. High above, all light and shadow and rich in carving, is the massive roof that Richard the Second put over the great hall. From the roof the light slants down in clear, straight beams, unclouded by any dust, and gathers in a pool at one place. There lies the coffin of the King.

The oak of Sandringham is hidden beneath the rich golden folds of the Standard. The slow flicker of the candles touches gently the gems of the Imperial Crown, even the ruby that King Henry wore at Agincourt. It touches the deep purple of the velvet cushion and the cool white flowers of the only wreath that lies upon the flag. How moving can such simplicity be. How real the tears of those who pass and see it, and come out again, as they do at this moment in un-broken stream, to the cold dark night and a little privacy for their thoughts.

Who can know what they are thinking? Does that blind man whom they lead so carefully down the thick carpet, sense around him the presence of history? Does he know that kings and queens have feasted here and stood their trial and gone to death? And that little woman with an air-man by her side—does she feel the ghosts that must be here in the shadows of the hall? The men and the women of those tumultuous days of long ago, of Chaucer, Essex, Anne Boleyn, Charles and Cromwell, Warren Hastings and those early Georges? Or does she, and do all those other seventy thousand of the nation, who will have passed through this day alone, think only of the sixth George: the faithful George who lies there now, guarded by the living statues of his officers and Gentlemen at Arms and Yeomen of the Guard? For in the few seconds that are all that can be given to each subject to pass by his dead King, there is colour and splen-dour and loveliness beyond compare.

I thought when I watched the bearers take the coffin into this hall yesterday that I had never seen a sight so touching. The clasped arms of the Grenadiers, the reverent care with which they lifted and carried their King. But I was wrong. For in the silent tableau of this lying-in-state there is a beauty that no movement can ever bring. He would be for-given who believed that these Yeomen of the Bodyguard, facing outwards from the corners of the catafalque, were carven statues of the Yeomen of the Tudor Henry's day. Could any living man, let alone a white, bearded man of eighty, be frozen into this immobility?

The faces of the two Gentlemen at Arms are hidden by the long white helmet plumes that have fallen about them like a curtain as they bowed their heads. Are they real, those faces, or do the plumes conceal two images of stone? And the slim, straight figures of the officers of the Household Brigade, hands poised lightly on their arms reversed, what sense of pride and honour holds their swords so still that not one gleam of light shall be reflected from a trembling blade?

Never safer, better guarded, lay a sleeping King than this, with a golden light to warm his resting-place and the muffled tread of his devoted people to keep him company. They come from a mile away in the night, moving pace by pace in hours of waiting, come into the silent majesty of the scene and, as silently, leave again.

Two hundred thousand may come to Westminster this week, but for every one of them there will be a thousand scattered about the world who cannot come, but who may be here in their thoughts at this moment. They will know that the sorrow of one man, one woman, or one child that passes by the King in London is their sorrow too.

For how true tonight of George the Faithful is that single sentence spoken by an unknown man of his beloved father: "The sunset of his death tinged the whole world's sky."

14

AT THE CATAFALQUE

AMONG the multitudes who filed into British Embassies all over the world to sign the visitors' book as a mark of personal mourning and respect was a Turkish naval rating. In the British Embassy in Istanbul he not only signed his name but added in English: "I am very sorry for the death of King George. May Queen Elizabeth bring you brightness and happiness."

I thought of that simple tribute and prayer from a foreign sailor sixteen hundred miles away as I looked down upon the impressive scene in St. George's Chapel, Windsor: the chapel of the Knights of the Garter that I had seen warm and alive with the richness and colour of ceremonial robes and pageantry, and which was now sombre and subdued, a muted symphony of black and white and half-tones, set off by the flushed beauty of the honey-coloured stone pillars and walls which, no longer dazzled by the splendour of scarlet and ermine, had come starkly into their own.

A pace in front of her mother, the Queen stood facing the catafalque, a lone, slender figure weighed down in black. Her face showed white through her veil and she looked very young, younger by far than her twenty-five years—the age, incidentally, at which her Tudor namesake had also ascended the throne.

In that intensely moving ritual one could feel for the official, so carried away that he forgot his cue and put the bowl of earth into the Queen's hands too soon. She held it uncertainly, as if all the natural bewilderment of her feelings had suddenly surfaced, and for a moment she seemed at a loss. Then she realised the mistake, and returned the bowl to the official to receive it again at the proper place in the service.

Almost imperceptibly the catafalque, bare now of the Crown and Regalia which had been replaced by the small crimson silk square of the King's Colour of the King's Company, Grenadier Guards, began to sink. The Archbishop spoke the words of the committal and the Queen performed the last rite for her father. From the golden bowl she scattered over the coffin earth gathered from Frogmore, where Queen Victoria lies with her beloved Prince Consort, as the mortal remains of George the Sixth vanished into the vault below to join the company of his father and grandfather, George V and Edward VII; the father of the first Queen Elizabeth, Henry VIII, sharing for some unknown reason the grave of Charles I; and those two mortal enemies of a lifetime, Henry VI of Lancaster and Edward IV of York, who found in death the peace of a common resting-place.

The voices of the choir soared into the hymn, "The strife is o'er, the battle done." The Queen curtsyed, and then turned slowly away and went out in procession to face the battles of her own reign.

Historically she was the fourth sovereign of the House of Windsor, and the fortieth since the Norman Conquest. She was the twelfth sovereign of Great Britain as legally constituted by the Act of Union between England and Scotland in 1707, although the Scots King James VI had adopted the title King of Great Britain a hundred years before, when he became James I of England. James wore, in fact, two crowns. He was King of England and King of Scots. He had of course been crowned as such in Scotland before he ever came to England, but his successors, Charles I and Charles II, were also crowned in Scotland as well as in England. It was not until the Act of Union that the two Crowns united in one Crown of Great Britain, just as the Scots Parliament merged into West-minster.

There were therefore substantial legal grounds for the pro-test by some Scots authorities against the Queen's accession as Queen Elizabeth the Second. Her namesake was Queen of England only: she herself was, in fact, the first Queen Elizabeth to be Queen of Great Britain. Apart from the practical con-siderations of simplicity of reference for future historians in distinguishing between our own Queen and her illustrious forebear of England, the nomenclature "Queen Elizabeth the Second" followed the practice adopted in the case of her uncle and great-grandfather. By the same reasoning that inspired the protest in the case of our own Queen's title, they should have been styled respectively Edward II and Edward I of Great Britain instead of Edward VIII and Edward VII.

To her peoples at large, however, the question of style of title was of far less import than the human side of the Crown, the personality of the Queen. What mattered in the eyes of her subjects was the irrefutable fact that Queen Elizabeth the Second was, as Mr. Churchill summed up, a fair and youthful figure, princess, wife, and mother, the "heir to all our tradi-tions and glories, never greater than in her father's day, and to all our perplexities and dangers, never greater in peace-time than now. She is also heir to our united strength and loyalty."

In that last inheritance of united strength and loyalty lies the promise of the new reign. Though the world is sorely vexed and troubled, and the country at home ridden with a domestic strife that is the inevitable outcome of shortage, the Crown has never gleamed more brightly. No sovereign has ascended a throne more securely based and with such inspiring assurance from the knowledge of the impregnable place she has already won in the hearts of her peoples.

The historian, J. R. Green, wrote of the first Elizabeth's accession: "Never had the fortunes of England sunk to a lower ebb than at the moment when Elizabeth mounted the Throne. . . . England's one hope lay in the character of her Queen."

Once again the fortunes of England are low, but in the character of the Queen how much greater is the advantage with which the second Elizabethan era begins. Her character is well known to all; it is the product of a happy childhood, based on the highest ethical and Christian principles, and secure in the knowledge of family love and unity.

By contrast, the first Elizabeth, with the lusty, imperious Henry VIII as her father and the scheming Anne Boleyn for mother, was not perhaps without some qualification for the title, "The daughter of the devil," which the Spanish ambassador bestowed upon her. In mitigation she could offer evidence of a childhood that would make most of the twentieth-century's broken homes to which young criminals' delinquencies are so often attributed seem highly respectable. In a bawdy atmosphere of suspicion and intrigue, where justice struck swiftly and without mercy, Elizabeth Tudor lived constantly under the shadow of the axe, an axe that had robbed her of both her mother and her first suitor, Thomas Seymour, and was never far from her own neck. She knew a grim, unhappy childhood and youth which fostered the development of her wiles and cunning, qualities without which she might never have survived to succeed to the throne. The wiles and cunning subsequently stood England in good stead as she played Spain and France against one another, maintaining a balance of power in Europe, until finally England was united in a national consciousness and was strong enough to meet force with force.

15

THE CONSTITUTION

IN his diary for November 12th, 1918, the Earl of Oxford referred to the Thanksgiving Service at St. Paul's Cathedral, which was attended by King George V and Queen Mary:

"I sat next Lady Lansdowne," he recorded, "and as one after another of our royalties were led up the Nave, I said to her, 'How long do you think this will last?'

" 'About fifty minutes,' she replied, imagining I was referring to the Service and not the Institution. 'I see that they have got rid of eight kings in Germany in the course of the last two or three days and there are more to follow.' "

Today the number of crowned heads has dwindled to such an extent that the remark attributed to ex-King Farouk of Egypt, latest recruit to the ranks of monarchs in exile, that there would soon be only five kings left—the kings of Spades, Hearts, Clubs and Diamonds, and the King of England—has become almost a reality.

The strength of the British monarchy and the British Constitution lies in the unwritten law. Throughout the centuries the principle and practice of the Constitution and the Crown's place in the Constitution have developed sometimes by accident, sometimes by intent. Part of the Constitution is defined in statutes, part can be found in decisions at law; much of it depends entirely upon tradition, custom, and practice.

The terms of the British Constitution have never been written out in one legal document, as is the case, for instance, in the United States. There the American Constitution was framed by Benjamin Franklin and his associates in 1788 as the basis of the federal government of the United States and the text, with amendments, is used by the Supreme Court for interpreting whether legislation is constitutional or not.

Nor has there been any attempt, as there was in France, to qualify to the letter the powers and authority of the Crown. Here again some of the Crown's powers have been defined by statutes, but in the true sense the royal prerogative is vested in the common law, the unwritten law of the realm. The word "prerogative" means the rights of the sovereign, who is theoretically subject to no restriction. Today the prerogative is generally accepted as embracing all the powers and privileges that the Crown derives from ancient usage and from the custom of the nation.

The nearest attempt at laying down an English Constitution was the Instrument of Government drawn up and put into force by Cromwell and his Army during the Commonwealth, but this was rescinded after the Restoration and has had no lasting influence upon the Constitution, which continues as always to develop in its own malleable way, building and modelling upon the past, modifying and adding to the old. In 1872, Professor E. A. Freeman wrote of the growth of the English Constitution:

The continued national life of the people, notwithstanding foreign conquests and internal revolutions, has remained unbroken for fourteen hundred years. At no moment has the tie between the present and the past been wholly rent asunder; at no moment have Englishmen sat down to put together a wholly new Constitution, in obedience to some dazzling theory. Each step in our growth has been the natural consequence of some earlier step; each change in our Law and Constitution has been, not the bringing in of anything wholly new, but the development and improvement of something that was already old. Our progress has in some ages been faster, in others slower; at some moments we have seemed to stand still, or even to go back; but the great march of political development has never wholly stopped; it has never been permanently checked since the days when the coming of the Teutonic conquerors first began to change Britain into England.

The passage is as applicable today as it was in Queen Victoria's time. The Constitution is as much a living thing as the nation that it serves, possessing the same endowment of regular growth and expansion. With no rigid pattern to be followed uncompromisingly, the Crown has never become a hardened mould presenting to any generation the same clear-cut conception on a "take it or leave it" basis. The individual sovereign has been able to bring his own interpretation of the influence of the Crown in the affairs of the nation, and upon the sovereign's personal discretion has rested the popularity and even the continued existence of the throne. Thus, although on the one hand the lack of restriction on its rights has made the Crown immeasurably powerful, the absence of any rigid rules has also provided a flexibility with which it has been able to adapt itself to meet changing circumstances. Outdated conventions, inconvenient practices have quietly been forgotten. New customs to meet contemporary needs have been adopted just as quietly. The result is that, throughout the centuries, the

Crown has imperceptibly accomplished the metamorphosis from owning the people to belonging to them.

At the time of our own Queen's accession some newspapers modelled their explanation of her actual powers upon Walter Bagehot's interpretation of the scope of the Royal Prerogative. In his book on the Constitution in 1868 Bagehot wrote of Queen Victoria:

> She could disband the Army (by law she cannot engage more than a certain number of men, but she is not obliged to engage any men); she could dismiss all the officers, from the General Commanding-in-Chief downwards; she could dismiss all the sailors too: she could sell off all our ships-of-war and all our naval stores; she could make a peace by the sacrifice of Cornwall and begin a war for the conquest of Brittany. She could make every citizen in the United Kingdom, male or female, a peer; she could make every parish in the United Kingdom a "University"; she could dismiss most of the civil servants, and she could pardon all offenders. In a word, the Queen could by Prerogative upset all the action of civil government within the Government; could disgrace the Nation by a bad war or peace, and could, by disbanding our forces, whether land or sea, leave us defence-less against foreign nations.

Queen Victoria was not amused. "Oh, the wicked man, to write such a story!" she is reported to have exclaimed. "Surely my people do not believe him?"

What is overlooked in conjecturing these fantastic impro-babilities as within the right of the Queen is the fact that it is unconstitutional for her to act at all except through or with the advice of her ministers, and consequently with the will of the people. From the earliest days the sovereign has needed the agreement and assistance of his subjects to put his powers effectively into operation. He began by calling together his most powerful barons into a council to help him in money matters, in providing an army and in civil administration. Subsequently the smaller landowners, and then the burgesses, representatives of the chartered boroughs, were added to the council. Simon de Montfort is often credited with being the founder of the House of Commons, because in 1265 he summoned a national assembly of knights from certain towns and shires and a large number of clergy to discuss the question of money supplies for the king. The birth of parliament as we know today really began thirty years later, however, when Edward I established the Model Parliament of "those who pray, those who fight, those who work"—the clergy, the barons, and the commons, the three estates of the realm. At last representatives of the organised communities of shires and towns—*les communes*, from which the House of Commons derives its name—were meeting regularly to approve taxation to meet the expenses of State, and to add their own support to the statutes of the king, administered through politically established courts of law which were set up at Westminster.

When Henry IV of Lancaster deposed Richard II he announced he would rule by "common advice, counsel, and consent" of "honourable, wise, and discreet persons of his kingdom," and his reign drew from the nineteenth-century historian, Bishop Stubbs, the comment: "Never before and never again for more than two hundred years were the Commons so strong as they were under Henry IV."

The consent of subject as a means of government may have

taken two hundred years to develop into practice, but the principle was established not only as an occasional custom but also as a legal opinion. Sir John Fortescue, who had been Chief Justice of England, wrote early in Edward IV's reign in his *De laudibus Legum Angliæ* (In Praise of the Laws of England):

As the head of the body natural cannot change its nerves and sinews, cannot deny to the several parts their proper energy, their due proportion and aliment of blood, neither can a king who is head of the body politic change the laws thereof, nor take away from the people what is theirs by right, against their consent. Thus you have the formal institution of every political kingdom, from whence you may guess at the power which a king may exercise with respect to the laws and subject. For he is appointed to protect his subjects in their lives, properties and laws; for this very end and purpose he has the delegation of power from the people and he has no just claim to any other power but this.

In short, to use Fortescue's oft-quoted summing-up of the position between sovereign and subject that remains the fundamental basis of the Constitution: "He [the King] can neither make any alteration or change in the laws of the realm without the consent of his subjects, nor burden them against their wills with strange impositions."

In practice, the exercise of the royal prerogative has developed into an instrument for protecting the rights of the people and ensuring that their will prevails. There is one particularly notable example of this development well within living memory. When the House of Lords rejected the Parliament Bill in 1910, Mr. Asquith, the Prime Minister, asked King

George V to create up to five hundred peers, if necessary, to ensure that the Bill would pass through the Lords when it was reintroduced. The Parliament Bill provided that after a Bill had passed through the House of Commons three times it should receive the Royal Assent and become law, notwithstanding a third rejection by the Lords. As this meant the transfer of power from the Lords to the Commons, whose will, once the Parliament Bill was law, must ultimately prevail, King George V decided that the final decision should rest with the people. He therefore gave a pledge that if the Government were returned at the general election he would accept the advice of using his prerogative to ensure the passing into law of the Parliament Bill. As it happened, the threat was sufficient, and the Parliament Bill passed through the House of Lords on its second introduction without the necessity of creating the new peers.

To understand the position that Queen Elizabeth occupies today in the life of this and "all her other realms" let me, not under any pretext as a constitutional lawyer but as a lay commentator, turn back for a moment the pages of history.

The origin of kingship is lost in the dim mists of the past. Two early cavemen, perhaps, were engaged in a mortal struggle when a third stayed them with a less drastic alternative to their dispute. The fame of the arbitrator's wisdom passed from mouth to mouth. Others began to bring him their problems and seek his advice. The status of a wise man, a leader, had come into being. Men began to look outside the immediate confines of their own family circles and acknowledged the leadership of one man, a chief under whom families became united into a tribe.

Through war, both as a result of direct conquest and also by

Walking in the garden

Being welcomed by President Truman in Washington, November 1951

amalgamation either to wage war or to resist attack, a sense of racial and national unity developed and the power and influence of the chief, the king, increased correspondingly. Kinship was extending to kingship. Following the principle of the early tribal chieftains who were chiefs of tribes, not territories, so the first kings acknowledged as such in our history were kings of people and not domains. Egbert, for instance, who began his reign in A.D. 827, claimed to be the first "King of the English."

Even then the theory was established that the king should act only in conjunction with his advisers—in Anglo-Saxon times the Great Council known as the Witan, which comprised various officials, nobles, bishops, and king's thegns, a landowning class ranking between the hereditary nobles and the ordinary freeholders. The Saxon king had absolute powers, but the exercise of them was checked by the necessity of acting through or with the Witan, and normally also by a natural disinclination not to offend the custom of his race. The Witan, in electing the King, confined their choice to members of the royal family, which was considered to be descended from gods. Though the field of choice was so limited, the elective nature of the monarchy and the practice of consultation with the Witan combined to make the king to some extent representative of his peoples, responsible for justice, law and order, the preservation of peace, and their protection in time of war. Nothing so unites a nation as threat of invasion, and the recurring attacks by the Danes did much to increase the power of the throne. Finally, Canute's defeat of Edmund Ironside caused the Witan to go beyond the range of royal birth and elect Canute as their king. This departure from custom resulted in so much strife and quarrelling over Canute's successors that the Saxon monarchy was saved from disintegration only by the Norman Conquest. Even William the Conqueror, although he had won his crown by force, was loud in his proclamation that it was his rightful inheritance, a claim without any foundation because William I was the illegitimate son of Robert of Normandy and a tanner's daughter. The theory of hereditary right as the most convenient method of ensuring a stable and peaceable succession was already taking shape.

Both the hereditary principle and the Crown itself were vastly strengthened by William's application of the feudal system, which provided him not only with a self-supporting administration but also with a trained army scattered throughout the country and ready for immediate action in the event of emergency, on much the same lines as the twentieth-century's territorial force. Under the feudal system all land was held on lease from the Crown in return for the supply each year of a specified number of warriors for so many days' service. This made the baronage entirely dependent upon the Crown, whose hold upon the loyalty and service of every great landowner was strengthened by personal relationship and individual contract. The landowners who held their land direct from the king as tenants-in-chief could in turn sub-let on a feudal tenure, but William took the precaution of requiring that every vassal, no matter from whom he held his land, should owe above the fealty to his immediate lord a prime allegiance and military service direct to the Crown. All vassals thus became king's men, and the threat that they might at any time be mobilised by their barons against the Crown was nullified.

The feudal system of inheritance also served to secure the power of the Crown. Had property been shared equally amongst heirs it would quickly have distintegrated into numerous small estates and become impracticable for the Crown to control. By establishing as sole legal heir the eldest son, who like his father would continue to hold the land on a military tenure, the Crown's hold over the country continued un-diminished. Further, if a tenant-in-chief had no heir, the property passed into the Crown's personal possession. This automatic inheritance of property, together with other acquisitions by confiscation for misdemeanours, made the sovereign increasingly powerful and, consequently, on his death, his eldest son, to whom the property passed intact under the same system of inheritance that applied to everyone else. By reason of the power which the eldest son of the king accordingly inherited, the elective character of the succession to the throne began to give place to the principle of hereditary right.

The change was a gradual process, and for four centuries the succession varied between those whose claims lay in descent and those who occupied the throne by "election" as a process which developed into title by Act of Parliament. Generally the success of the claim to the throne depended also upon a strong arm, but by 1216 the hereditary principle was sufficiently recognised to allow the accession of the nine-year-old Henry III. Whether a sovereign wore the Crown by parliamentary title or through direct inheritance, he generally took pains to establish himself as king according to both viewpoints on the monarchy. If the throne came to him by descent, he passed an Act of Parliament to confirm his title. If he were elected to the throne, he was just as eager to establish his hereditary claim as well.

Not until the claims of the rival branches of the Plantagenet family, the houses of York and Lancaster, had been finally settled by the Wars of the Roses with the victory of Henry

Tudor—Henry VII (who promptly united the two factions by marrying Elizabeth of York, the daughter of Edward IV)—was the succession to the throne settled on an hereditary basis. Though he claimed the throne both by "judgment of God in the field" and hereditary right, Henry VII, too, sought a parliamentary title and signed an Act of Settlement settling the Crown on him and his heirs.

With Henry VII's accession conditions grew more stable. The rival houses of York and Lancaster had been so equally matched that the struggle of the Roses had cost them and their supporters dear. The nobility generally was crippled and impoverished and no longer constituted a danger to the Crown, and taking advantage of the weakness of the aristocracy Henry Tudor consolidated and strengthened the position of the monarchy.

Bolingbroke wrote of this period in his *Letters on the Study of History*:

> We neither laid waste our own or other countries any longer, and wise laws and a wise government changed insensibly the manners and gave a new turn to the spirit of our people. We were no longer the freebooters we had been. The arts of peace prevailed among us. We became husbandmen, manufacturers, and merchants and we emulated neighbouring nations in literature.

In a state of stabilised society and government the law of hereditary succession was at last established in practice. The claims of both Lancastrians and Yorkists were united in Henry VII's son, and when in due course he was crowned as Henry VIII it was the first time in a hundred years that the succession to the throne had not been disputed. With the subsequent

Daily Graphic Picture Service

Picture Post

Canadian Tour, 1951

The Lying-in-State of King George VI, February 1952

exception of the controversial case of James Stuart, hereditary monarchy had come to stay.

During the past century, particularly, the hereditary nature of our monarchy has been the subject for attack from some quarters. The arguments generally presented by the critics are that hereditary monarchy is contrary to present-day conceptions of equality and freedom of opportunity for all, and that it is neither logical nor just that accident of birth should bring an individual to so exalted a place in the realm and in the affairs of State.

Hereditary monarchy does, of course, set a premium on chance, and the principle has brought us our share of bad sovereigns. In the days of absolute monarchy, a weak king meant a weak government and a bad king a bad government: both, however, were preferable to no government at all. The interregnum between the demise of one king and the accession of the next had already provided experience of conditions when government and law and order ceased to exist. Such a state of affairs would undoubtedly have followed the transfer of government from monarch to the baronage, who were invariably far more preoccupied with their own squabbles, jealousies, and personal interests than with the affairs of the nation as a whole.

So long as the succession to the throne was not cut and dried, there was always strife or threat of strife. Hereditary monarchy simplified the problem that arose with almost every new reign and stabilised both the Crown and the peace of the nation. Today, with constitutional monarchy so exacting and specialised a role, the advantages of an hereditary monarchy lie particularly in the concentrated training that the heir or heiress receives from childhood, and also in the Crown's absolute impartiality. This is made possible only by birth into a family that is kept religiously free of party or any other interest that might influence the choice of a sovereign, as if, for example, the monarchy were elective like the presidency of the United States.

Weakness in any system of government lies not so much in the institution as in the fallibility of the individual. At their extremes both monarchy and republicanism, however it may be named, can lead to tyranny and abuse. Russia knew the autocracy of the Czar, but the substitution of the "peoples' government" has led to a similar despotism in the present-day régime. In Germany, Kaiser Wilhelm II oppressed by right of birth, whilst Adolf Hitler drew his unrestrained powers from the State.

In the British Crown, envied by many a republican country unable to achieve a stable government and living amidst political chaos, there has developed through the centuries a constitutional administration embodying the best of monarchy and democracy and pursuing always a course of moderation, adaptation, and compromise. The peculiarly British system of a limited hereditary monarchy has become an anchor of stability guaranteeing the steadfast continuation of the Constitution and the national way of life amidst all the inconstancy and turbulence of the present century.

As for the privileged luxury of the position bestowed by accident of birth, the first Queen Elizabeth, who ruled where Queen Elizabeth the Second now reigns and who had more personal rewards to reap from her office both in power and material satisfaction as well as in wealth, said in November 1601, after forty-two years on the throne:

"To be a King and wear a crown is a thing more glorious to them that see than it is pleasant to them that bear it."

16

LAW AND THE SOVEREIGN

THE practice of the Anglo-Saxons in electing their kings from amongst members of the royal family only was no doubt largely the result of the superstitious belief that the royal family were descended from gods. The Norman feudal system placed monarchy on the basis of a contract between king and subject. As the feudal system of administration died out, some other tie of duty to the Crown was felt necessary to take the place of the feudal bond. Hereditary monarchy suggested the answer in its own principle of inheritance from father to son. In the past the monarchy had equipped itself with a supernatural origin. In a Christian England the Crown turned again to a superhuman agency and imposed the doctrine of the Divine Right of Kings, a theory which maintained that a king was the appointed representative of God, from Whom he derived his supreme authority and to Whom alone he was responsible.

At the opening of the first parliament after his accession to the English throne, James I gave an indication of the policy he intended to initiate as the Stuart theory of monarchy when he thanked members for receiving him "in this seat which God, by my birthright and lineal descent, had, in the fullness of time, provided for me." Later, in 1609, he elaborated on the doctrine of the Divine Right in this address to parliament:

Kings are justly called gods because they exercise a manner of resemblance of Divine power upon earth. For if you will consider the attributes of God you shall see how they agree in the person of a King. God hath power to create or destroy, make or unmake, at His pleasure, to give life or send death, to judge all and to be accountable to none. And this like power have Kings. They make and unmake their subjects, they have power of raising up and casting down, of life and death, they are judges over all their subjects and in all cases, yet accountable to none but God. They have power to exalt low things and abase high things and to make of their subjects like men at chess.

The immunity that Divine Right was intended to give the monarchy was short-lived. It did not save Charles I from losing his head or James II his Crown. In practice, the doctrine suffered its death-knell in the Bill of Rights, which curbed a monarch's tendencies towards despotism and prevented his arbitrary interference with law and subject. When the last of the Stuart monarchs, Anne, came to the throne, she proclaimed that not even in theory did she adhere to the belief of the Divine Right.

One superhuman ability, older than the doctrine of Divine Right and dating back to Edward the Confessor, was the power attributed to a monarch of miraculously curing scrofula, a glandular disease then known as "the king's evil." Contemporary records refer to a large number of cures resulting from this treatment of "touching," in which the monarch, sitting in state with his clergy, physicians, and nobles, laid hands on the patients' afflicted parts. No doubt the psychological effect of contact between subject and sovereign had much to do with these reported cures; perhaps also they were achieved by means, the nature of which is still controversial and generally incomprehensible, similar to the spirit-healing cases of today.

Although Anne had denounced the theory of the Divine Right, she apparently considered herself imbued with miraculous powers of healing, for she revived the custom of "touching" which had been discontinued by her brother-in-law, William III. Amongst the patients "touched" by Anne was Dr. Samuel Johnson, at the time an infant of two and a half. In his case, however, there was no magic cure in the royal touch, for the famous lexicographer remained badly afflicted by the disease throughout his life. Patients generally were not likely to be too critical of the royal treatment, however, because whatever the results there was consolation to be had in the touch-piece, a gold coin attached to a white ribbon, which was hung round the neck of each patient as a part of the ritual. Queen Anne was the last sovereign to "touch." Her successor, George I of Hanover, ridiculed the notion that any miraculous powers of healing might lie in his hands, and a practice that had lasted well over six hundred years finally came to an end.

The Stuarts claimed that the king could do no wrong because he acted in accordance with divine will, but throughout the centuries the oft-quoted maxim has always applied in some truth to our monarchy. Sir William Blackstone, the eminent eighteenth-century lawyer and judge, wrote in his *Commentaries on the Laws of England*: "The king is not only incapable of doing wrong but even of thinking wrong; he can never mean to do an improper thing; in him is no folly or weakness."

The principle that the sovereign can do no wrong—the prerogative of perfection as it is often called—applies equally to Queen Elizabeth today, but on different grounds from those which James Stuart claimed. Her powers as sovereign are exercised not by herself personally but through the ministers who bear sole responsibility for all actions taken in the Queen's name. As the law does not acknowledge the existence of any circumstances in which the sovereign might commit or institute an unlawful act, it is inadmissible for the servants of the Crown to plead in excuse for a misdemeanour that it was committed by royal command. Rather than giving the sovereign unbridled licence and independence, the assignment of complete personal responsibility from sovereign to official has the opposite effect. An official who knows that he will bear the full consequences of the Crown's action is naturally going to take pains to resist any attempt upon the part of the sovereign to perpetrate any deed of doubtful legality.

This principle of ministerial responsibility, which has become an inherent part of the British Constitution, first saw practical demonstration when parliament sought redress against Charles I's rule by impeaching his ministers—the Duke of Buckingham in 1626, and subsequently the Earl of Strafford and Archbishop Laud.

"The laws of England have taught us that kings cannot command ill or unlawful things," said Sir Dudley Digges, presenting the case against Buckingham. "And whatsoever ill events succeed, the executioners of such designs must answer for them."

Sir John Eliot went further and stated the principle that an official should resist any royal commands that he knew to be unlawful. "My lords, I will say that if His Majesty himself were pleased to have consented, or to have commanded, which I cannot believe, yet this could no way satisfy for the Duke, or make any extenuation of the charge, for it was the duty of his place to have opposed it by his prayers, and to have interceded

with His Majesty to make known the dangers, the ill consequences that might follow."

Charles fought for Buckingham and attempted to assume
responsibility. "And for some particulars wherewith he hath
been pressed, however he hath made his answer, certain it is
that I did command him to do what he hath done therein," the
King wrote to the House of Commons.

Had the King's assumption of full responsibility succeeded,
it would have meant that with his royal person inviolate and
unanswerable in any court of law—the court that subsequently
brought him to trial and execution was without any authority
and quite unconstitutional—no redress would have been possible for any actions by the Crown. As it was, parliament's victory, confirmed fourteen years later by the impeachment of
Strafford and Laud, brought a constitutional remedy through
the case of ministerial responsibility.

This principle was categorically restated in the reign of
Queen Anne by the Earl of Rochester who, in a debate on a
motion of censure against the government for their handling
of the war of the Spanish Succession, said that "for several
years they had been told that the Queen was to answer for
everything; but he hoped that time was over; that according
to the fundamental Constitution of the Kingdom the Ministers
are accountable for all, and therefore he hoped that nobody
would—nay, nobody durst—name the Queen in this debate."

Queen Anne, always concerned that no one should be mis-
taken into thinking that she was to be hectored or frightened
into a compliance because she was a woman, was the last
sovereign to attend debates in the House of Lords, and she had
no scruples about utilising her presence to influence policy. She
was also the last sovereign to make use of the veto. The power

of veto still lies with our Queen Elizabeth, but she could execute it constitutionally only upon the advice of her ministers. As all Bills brought before the Queen are those introduced and passed by her ministers they are hardly likely to advise her to veto their own measures, and it is most improbable that the Norman French phrase, "*Le Roy s'avisera*," by which the Royal Assent is withheld will be heard in the present reign. The power of veto is there, however, to be used as a last resort should an unforeseen development or sudden change in circumstances make it desirable for a government to abandon a Bill that has already passed through parliament. It was in such circumstances that Queen Anne exercised the veto in 1703 over the Scots Militia Bill. Whilst the Bill, passed by Parliament, was awaiting the royal assent, a Jacobite movement to restore the Stuarts was discovered in Scotland. With this new development the Bill might have become a danger to the Crown and Hanoverian succession, and Anne was accordingly advised by her ministers to apply the veto, which killed the Bill as effectively as if it had been thrown out by parliament.

George I of Hanover, who followed Anne to the throne, understood practically no English. He was unable to follow what was taking place at the meetings of his ministers and decided in any case to stay away, thus starting a custom that has since been followed. His absence brought the need for a minister to preside in his place—a Prime Minister—and, without in any way interfering with the prerogative of the Crown, gave also further practical evidence of the sovereign's freedom from responsibility for the acts in his name.

Hitherto the king had possessed a definite say in the government of his realm, ruling, in fact, through his ministers. Now, by the accident of a German king who knew no English, the

The Queen on a visit to Edinburgh, July 1952

Picture Post

The Queen taking the Salute at the Trooping the Colour, 1952

tables began to turn, and it became the ministers who governed through the instrument of the Crown—the basis of our present-day constitutional monarchy. Opposition to this new conception came from George III, who was not satisfied with reigning but wanted to rule personally and independently of party government. He sought to achieve his aim by having corruptly returned to parliament members known as the "King's Friends," who voted to bring about his personal wishes. This corruption of the House of Commons by Crown patronage was ended by the Reform Bill of 1832, which also extended the franchise to include the middle and newly-rising industrial classes. The party returned to power was therefore directly representative of such a vast majority of people that it would have been difficult for any sovereign to resist such a pressure of national will. The Crown, in the person of William IV, however, made no attempt at resistance. Although he maintained a right to advise his ministers, he accepted the fact that popular opinion must prevail; that the Crown was the servant of the people. The loss of its executive powers was compensated by the increased stature and dignity that the Crown gained by its removal from party discord and all political responsibility.

The Crown still retained a right to be informed of its ministers' intentions: a right upon which Queen Victoria was most explicit in a message she sent to Lord Palmerston in 1850.

"The Queen requires," she wrote, "first, that Lord Palmerston will distinctly state what he proposes in a given case, in order that the Queen may know as distinctly to what she is giving her royal sanction. Secondly, having once given her sanction to a measure, that it be not arbitrarily altered or modified by the Minister. Such an act she must consider as failing in sincerity towards the Crown, and justly to be visited by the exercise of her constitutional rights of dismissing that Minister. She expects to be kept informed of what passes between him and the foreign ministers, before important decisions are taken based upon that intercourse; to receive the foreign despatches in good time, and to have the drafts for her approval sent to her in sufficient time to make herself acquainted with their contents before they must be sent off."

The recent Crown Proceedings Act of 1947 has brought a notable change in the application of the law that the king can do no wrong. Until the operation of this Act, ministers in their role of agents of the Crown enjoyed the same immunity from legal proceedings as the sovereign. In practice, if the individual responsible for an offence occurring in the normal work of the Crown could not be ascertained, the Crown nominated a defendant to avoid unfair operation of its legal immunity.

In 1946 the Crown nominated the army officer in charge of the area as defendant in a case arising out of injuries to children in a derelict minefield of which the Crown was the occupier. The Court, however, dismissed the case as no personal negligence upon the part of the officer could be proved, and the injured parties were left without any legal redress.

As a result of this new Act, proceedings can now be brought against the Crown in the shape of the appropriate Minister or government department, or alternatively the Attorney-General. Today the maxim that the sovereign can do no wrong applies only to the person of Queen Elizabeth herself.

17

THE RIGHTS OF THE SOVEREIGN

IN spite of the Civil War, the revolution against James II, and the various reformative measures introduced down the ages, not to deprive sovereignty but to safeguard against abuse of the Crown's unlimited authority, the powers and privileges vested in our Queen Elizabeth are intrinsically the same as those enjoyed by her ancestral queens, Mary, Elizabeth the First, Anne, and Victoria. The distinction between the powers of our own Queen and the first Elizabeth lies in their application. Sovereignty is exercised no longer by the Queen in person but by the Queen in Parliament, in which guise Queen Elizabeth is still the supreme executive and legislative authority. It is the Queen in Parliament who makes the laws, the Queen in the courts who interprets them, and the Queen in the various departments of the central government of the Crown who puts the laws into effect. The Queen is the personification of the State, the emblem of its dignity and unity. She is "the fountain of honour, the fountain of justice, the fountain of mercy." She is the Supreme Governor of the Established Church and the Commander-in-Chief of the Armed Forces.

One of Elizabeth Tudor's Secretaries of State, Sir Thomas Smith, wrote in 1583 that parliament "representeth and hath the power of the whole realm, both the head and body. For every Englishman is intended to be there present, either in person or by procuration and attorneys, of what pre-eminence, state, dignity, quality soever he be, from the prince, be he king or queen, to the lowest person of England, and the consent of the Parliament is taken to be every man's consent." If parliament be the body, then the Queen is both the spirit and architect of parliament, which she summons, prorogues, and dissolves.

It is the Queen's prerogative to declare war and make peace. It is she who negotiates treaties, receives foreign diplomats, and generally maintains international relations. The Queen appoints the leading officers of Church and State and creates corporations by the grant of charters.

One prime advantage that the prerogative possesses over the statutory powers of the Crown is the fact that there is no necessity for parliament to be consulted in advance about the use of the prerogative. This privilege is of particular value in matters relating to the armed forces, foreign affairs, honours, and appointments, which are not always suitable for discussion in the House. Parliament, however, has the right to criticise the use of the prerogative just as it can criticise any other act of administration by means of amendments to the Queen's Speech, questions to the minister, a proposal to reduce the minister's salary, a motion for the adjournment, formal resolution, or vote of censure.

Naturally in major matters, such as a declaration of war, no minister of the Crown would accept the responsibility of advising the sovereign to take such a step (although it would be constitutional for him to do so) until he had ascertained that he had the support of parliament and the nation. As with the statutory powers of the Crown, the royal prerogative is normally exercised upon the advice of the ministers, but it is generally agreed that there are two cases in which the Queen can exercise her prerogative without the advice or even against

Balmoral, September 1952

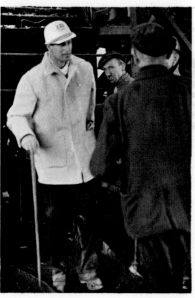

Four studies of the Duke of Edinburgh

the advice of her ministers. These are the selection of a Prime Minister where the leadership of a party returned to power is not definitely established, and the dissolution of parliament.

The obvious case in which the Queen might have to decide the premiership would be in the event of a coalition government. Again, if the Labour Party were to return to power mainly as a result of a campaign by Mr. Aneurin Bevan, for example, the Queen might be faced with the choice of inviting him or Mr. Attlee to form a government. Queen Victoria experienced a similar situation when Gladstone emerged from retirement to wage a successful campaign against the Conservatives. Actually Queen Victoria sent for Lord Hartington, the official leader of the Liberals, but he advised her to ask Gladstone to form a government.

If Mr. Churchill were to fall ill and resign his office the choice of his successor, if he were not already clearly defined, would lie with the Queen. Such a problem faced her grandfather, King George V, in 1923, when Mr. Bonar Law resigned because of ill health. There were two possible candidates for the vacant premiership, Lord Curzon, the Secretary of State for Foreign Affairs, and Mr. Stanley Baldwin, Chancellor of the Exchequer. King George V took pains to ensure that no personal inclinations should influence his choice.

"The King is in communication with those whose opinions His Majesty would naturally seek in the exceptional circumstances which precluded him from seeing and consulting the outgoing Premier," he announced.

Although the claims of Lord Curzon from the point of view of experience were the stronger, it was Mr. Baldwin who was called to the office, primarily because the Labour Party had no representatives in the House of Lords and it was desirable that the Prime Minister should meet the Opposition on the same ground. Since then the practice of selecting the Prime Minister from the House of Commons has been consistently followed, but it will have to continue uninterrupted for, perhaps, two hundred years before historians and constitutional lawyers regard George V's selection of Mr. Baldwin as establishing a new constitutional principle. If circumstances arose where Queen Elizabeth—and consequently the will of the people—thought it desirable to select a Premier from the House of Lords, there is no reason why she should not do so. Had Mr. Churchill been in the House of Lords instead of the Commons in 1940 when the nation was seeking a national figure of his calibre for the premiership, there is no reason to believe that his peerage would have disqualified him from office because of King George V's action seventeen years before. Such is the flexibility and value of the British Constitution.

The second personal prerogative of the sovereign, the right to use the royal discretion on the dissolution of parliament, is a thorny problem. The issue reached a climax of controversy in 1913 over the Home Rule for Ireland Bill, a measure considered in some quarters to be outside the government's mandate and against the temper of the people. As the government was not itself prepared to go to the country, it was widely suggested that King George V should exercise his prerogative and dissolve parliament before the Bill became law, in order that the nation should have an opportunity of expressing its opinion on the subject at a general election.

The Prime Minister in question, Mr. Asquith, prepared a memorandum on the sovereign's position, in which after admitting the right and duty of a constitutional monarch to point out objections against a course advised by his ministers

and, if he thought fit, to suggest an alternative policy, he
stated:

But in the end the Sovereign always acts upon the advice
which Ministers, after full deliberation and (if need be)
reconsideration, feel it their duty to offer. They give that
advice well knowing that they can, and probably will, be
called to account for it by Parliament.

The Sovereign undoubtedly has the power of changing
his advisers, but it is relevant to point out that there has been,
during the past 130 years, one occasion only on which the
King has dismissed the Ministry which still possessed the
confidence of the House of Commons. This was in 1834,
when William IV (one of the least wise of British monarchs)
called upon Lord Melbourne to resign . . . but the proceedings were neither well-advised nor fortunate. . . . The authority of the Crown was disparaged. . . .

Nothing can be more important, in the best interests of
the Crown and of the country, than that a practice, so long
established and so well justified by experience, should remain
unimpaired. It frees the occupant of the Throne from all
personal responsibility for the acts of the Executive and the
legislature. It gives force and meaning to the old maxim that
"the King can do no wrong." So long as it prevails, however
objectionable particular Acts may be to a large section of his
subjects, they cannot hold him in any way accountable. If, on
the other hand, the King were to intervene on one side, or in
one case—which he could only do by dismissing his ministers in *de facto* possession of a Parliamentary majority—he
would be expected to do the same on another occasion, and
perhaps for the other side. Every Act of Parliament of the

first order of importance would be regarded as bearing the personal imprimatur of the Sovereign. He would, whether he wished it or not, be dragged into the arena of party politics; and at a dissolution following such a dismissal of ministers as has just been referred to, it is no exaggeration to say that the Crown would become the football of contending factions.

The Times for September 8th, 1913, took the view that "Legally there is no question that under the Constitution there are certain reserved rights of the Crown; but they are atrophied by long disuse." Many experts of the Constitution protested that there was no reason why the privileges of the Crown should die just because they were not being used. In particular, Sir William Anson replied to *The Times* with a letter that has been generally accepted as summing-up the constitutional position on the personal prerogative of dissolution.

"Our only safeguard . . ." he wrote, "is to be found in the exercise of the prerogatives of the Crown. I am not ready to admit that, under such circumstances, these prerogatives have been atrophied by disuse: but, on the other hand, they can be exercised only under certain conditions which those who write on the subject are apt to ignore. For every public act of the King his Ministers must accept responsibility. . . . It really comes to this, that if the King should determine, in the interests of the people, to take a course which his Ministers disapprove, he must either convert his Ministers to his point of view or, before taking action, must find other Ministers who agree with him."

We may hope that the second Elizabethan age will subject the Queen to no such crisis, and that the Crown's personal prerogatives and rights may be left to lie peacefully undisturbed.

There is none the less comfort in the knowledge that the power is there to be brought out if necessary as a final resort to save the British Constitution and way of life. On such a thorny subject Queen Elizabeth has to guide her this sound advice from her great-great-grandmother, Queen Victoria, who wrote that the power of dissolving parliament was "a most valuable and powerful instrument in the hands of the Crown, but which ought not to be used except in extreme cases and with a certainty of success. To use this instrument and be defeated is a thing most lowering to the Crown and hurtful to the country."

With the powers of the House of Lords curtailed by the Parliament Bills of 1911 and 1947, so that the upper chamber no longer has any authority over financial bills and can do no more than delay non-monetary bills for a maximum of twelve months, the royal prerogative has assumed an increasing importance as the final bastion of the Constitution. To preserve that Constitution is Queen Elizabeth's first responsibility, and it is for this purpose that the authority of the prerogative remains vested in her. In practice, of course, the prerogative is no longer a sovereign's privilege. It has become instead the privilege of the people, and the Queen is there to see that their rights are protected and that their will prevails. When it is not possible to ascertain the people's wishes directly upon any matter, then the Queen is constitutionally bound to give her wholehearted support and confidence to the party in power, the government of the day. That is the only opinion allowed her.

On one occasion a personal opinion on the policy of free trade was attributed to her great-grandfather, Edward VII. He replied immediately: "The King never expresses any opinion on political matters except on the advice of his responsible ministers, and therefore the statement must be inaccurate."

The Queen executes her formal acts of government in three ways: by Orders in Council, by Warrants, Commissions and Orders under the Sign Manual, and by Proclamations, Writs, Letters Patent, Charters, and other documents under the Great Seal of the Realm.

An Order in Council is a resolution passed by a meeting of her Privy Council and may concern a matter coming within either her prerogative or statutory powers. Under her prerogative, the Queen in Council may decide the colonial legislation, as in the case of the reconstitution of the Legislative Council of Mauritius in 1947. By Orders in Council, too, the Queen regulates the discipline and administration of the Crown departments.

Under the Sign Manual, the Queen signs with her own hand documents relating to appointments, instructions to governors of colonies, and also issues pardons. These warrants signed by the Queen are countersigned by the appropriate minister, who accepts the responsibility for the act. It was under a Sign Manual warrant that Queen Victoria exercised her prerogative to abolish the purchase of commissions in the Army when the House of Lords refused assent to Mr. Gladstone's Bill. It was by Warrant that Queen Elizabeth determined the precedence of her husband. The announcement in the *London Gazette* dated September 31st, 1952, stated:

The Queen has been graciously pleased by Warrant bearing date the 18th inst. to declare and ordain that His Royal Highness, Philip, Duke of Edinburgh, Knight of the Most Noble Order of the Thistle, Commander in the Royal Navy, shall henceforth upon all occasions and in all Meetings except where otherwise provided by Act of Parliament have, hold and enjoy Place, Pre-eminence and Precedence next to her Majesty.

(Sgd) G. R. Bellew, Garter King of Arms.

Previously he had been the most junior of the royal dukes and took precedence after the Dukes of Windsor and Gloucester. The exception referred to is the Duke of Edinburgh's position in the House of Lords, where he continues to rank as the junior duke. His precedence there could be changed only by Act of Parliament.

It is under the Great Seal, first used by Edward the Confessor and now kept in the custody of the Lord Chancellor, that the Queen issues proclamations of a state of war or emergency, or the dissolution of parliament. No one but the Queen under the Great Seal may issue proclamations, and these are restricted by constitutional usage to acts of the prerogative or to calling attention to the statutory law. Once a proclamation is published in the *London Gazette* it is as valid in law as an Act of Parliament. Under the Great Seal the Queen signs treaties with other nations and causes writs for parliamentary elections to be issued. By Letters Patent under the Great Seal titles are conferred, Royal Commissions are appointed, new offices are constituted, and provision is made for the government of colonies. It was by Letters Patent under the Great Seal that King George VI decreed that the children of the marriage between Princess Elizabeth and the Duke of Edinburgh should "at all time hold and enjoy the style, title, or attribute of Royal Highness and the titular dignity of Prince or Princess."

Often the ways in which the Queen's Pleasure may be expressed are interwoven. Thus parliament is dissolved by Proclamation, and an Order in Council commands the issue of the writs for the summoning of a new parliament; and apart from a few statutory exceptions a Sign Manual Warrant is necessary to authorise the use of the Great Seal.

There are many other incidental rights appertaining to the Queen. She decides what the Royal Arms shall be, and grants licences for their use. She approves the occasions on which salutes shall be fired and the number of guns that shall be used. All treasure trove belongs to the Queen; so do any whales or sturgeon caught within territorial waters and any white swans, provided they are wild and unmarked, frequenting open and common rivers. The Queen is the owner of the foreshore—the land between the high-water and low-water marks—and also of the sea-bed in all territorial waters throughout the Dominions. Hers is the sole right of printing, or granting licences to print, the Bible and Book of Common Prayer, and State documents. The building and supervision of harbours, the grant of markets and fisheries, the award of civil list pensions, the coinage, all come within the royal prerogative. Royal tours, receptions, formal meetings of the Council, the holding of investitures, the signing of an endless succession of State documents, the granting of audiences in infinite variety, the patronage of music, art, drama, literature, science, sport, charity, welfare, and almost every form of national activity— these are but some of the regular routine duties of the Queen.

The royal palaces, which belong to the nation and are the Queen's by tenure of the Crown only, are free of rates and taxes, but these are paid in full on her personal property, such as the Sandringham estate. If she were to fail to pay, however, there would be no means of recovery, as the Queen cannot be sued in her own courts. Though she may hold and buy private property, she is not permitted to rent from a subject. She has no vote, and it is unlikely that she will see in use the new home of her faithful Commons who, at the time that she attended debates as a princess, were still using the House of Lords. Not since 1642, when Charles I arrived with the intention of "pulling out by the ear" the Five Members—Pym, Hampden, Hazlerigg, Holles, and Strode—and arresting them for treason, has a sovereign entered the House of Commons. Since then, of course, it is the fear that the presence of the sovereign may hamper free discussion and influence decisions —Queen Anne certainly attended debates in the House of Lords with this deliberate intention—that has established the custom. Although the Queen summons parliament to advise her upon the government of the country, it is only in the form of Bills passed through the House that the advice is tendered her.

Greatest disability of all, however, that the wearing of the crown brings to Queen Elizabeth is the isolation from participation in normal everyday life, and the artificial atmosphere of constant deference that precludes natural conversation and frank expression of views in her presence. Queen Victoria once complained that she did not know what a railway ticket looked like. Careful preparation and training for the throne, with a remarkable freedom by constitutional standards to mix democratically with those who are now her subjects, have given Queen Elizabeth an awareness and understanding that will humanise the aloofness thrust upon her with the Crown. From her own experience she will always appreciate, as she said herself, exactly what goes on behind the scenes on the occasion of any royal visit or ceremony.

The formal fetters and remoteness of a sovereign's position are tempered further by the help of a consort upon whom the Constitution places no restraint from free-and-easy intercourse with the people. The status of Queen Consort is recognised and, although she is a subject, she enjoys certain rights and privileges, including the protection of her life and chastity by the law of treason. The position of husband of a Queen Regnant, however, is not prescribed in the British Constitution. He is simply a subject with no special privileges over any other subject, and it is thus in the role of intermediary between the Queen and her people that the Duke of Edinburgh is able to render unique and valuable service. From the Duke, Queen Elizabeth can obtain the ungilded truth about national affairs and the real views of the people. With the Duke, Her Majesty can discuss the problems of monarchy with a freedom and intimacy impossible in audiences with her ministers, however privileged.

It is said that the burden of monarchy falls doubly upon a Queen Regnant, who has to undertake not only the complete duties of a king but also those of a Queen Consort, which are invariably so feminine in character that they cannot be passed to her husband. The Duke of Edinburgh, however, has already fashioned his own role in relation to the Crown by relieving his wife of some of those duties which his position and sex enable him to carry out more thoroughly than the Queen could hope to do. Within the first weeks of the new reign he had put in hand a personal investigation of Britain's industry and scientific research, visiting collieries, heavy industries, the National Physical Laboratory, and Harwell. They were visits that went far beyond the formal reception committees and presentation of executives. In a manner denied to the Queen, he was able to piece together a comprehensive survey of the heart of British industry. Albert, the Prince Consort, sought to encourage industry from the top by inspiring the directors and manufacturers themselves. Philip, the Duke of Edinburgh, has chosen to tackle the job from the bottom. It was the men themselves that he talked to informally about their work and their problems, and he had no hesitation about going down the pits and watching the miners at work at the coal-face. In addition to the understanding that he was acquiring for himself, for the Queen, for the nation, his visits themselves proved valuable incentives to morale and production. His tour of the Lancashire coalfields, for instance, gave such an impetus to the miners that the pits in the area broke all production records in the ensuing weeks.

The Duke of Edinburgh subsequently summed up his impressions of his tours of industrial and research undertakings in a speech to the University of Wales, in which he named the forces of prosperity as science, craftsmanship, and labour, the "know-how," the ability and the will to work.

"First," he said, "I found there is a great wealth of scientific and technological knowledge ready to be used. Part of this store has been used with conspicuous success but, by and large, there is still a widespread disregard on the part of industry towards the use of scientific knowledge.

"Secondly, I relearned the lesson one learns quickly in the Services, that the quality of work and enthusiasm of work-people depends almost entirely on human relations.

"Thirdly, I am completely convinced that those who say that craftsmanship is dead are quite wrong. Given the tools, and it is the tools that have changed and not the men, British craftsmen are as far ahead as ever."

Since the reign of George V the Crown has become firmly settled as a national, social, and family institution. It is truly a nationalised service belonging to the people far more than any politically nationalised undertaking. Industries such as coal or transport, nationalised by Act of Parliament, are owned by the State; the Crown, above the State, has become the direct interest of the people themselves, protecting them if necessary from the machinations of the State in the shape of the political party in power. With that personal sense of ownership which no man feels towards the railways or the Bank of England, it is the human interest in the Crown that has become more important than ever. The firmly fixed conception of the Crown as a symbol and institution and an instinctive outlet of patriotism and idealism that borders on the verge of religion, makes it difficult for any king or queen to fail today as a sovereign. It is as a man or a woman that he or she might be found wanting. Queen Elizabeth has already given, from the days of her apprenticeship, ample proof that she will not fail in either respect, and it is undoubtedly in his application of his firm belief in human relations that the Duke of Edinburgh will succeed in extending still further the personal influence of the Queen, in bringing her still closer to her subjects and, ultimately, in making the monarchy even more democratic.

Already it is believed that the Duke harbours a wish for Prince Charles to receive a more liberal education than that which convention bestows upon the heir to the throne. The Duke himself, brought up under spartan conditions at Gordonstoun, near Elgin in Scotland, knew what is probably the most advanced system of reputable schooling in force today. There are seven basic rules of education at Gordonstoun:

1. The boys shall have opportunities for self-discovery.
2. That they shall meet with both triumph and defeat.
3. That they shall have opportunity for self-effacement in a common cause.

4. The provision of regular periods of silence.

5. Training of the imagination.

6. That games shall be regarded as important but not pre-dominant.

7. That the sons of the wealthy and powerful shall be freed from the weakening sense of privilege.

Possibly it is under some such system of education that he himself enjoyed that the Duke of Edinburgh, as a father, would like his son to develop. The objection in the past to the entry of heirs to the throne into a public school has always been that the future king requires to develop individuality, whereas a public school teaches the sinking of individuality in the team spirit.

It was to offset the effects of private tutors, although the up-bringing of royal children was traditionally more rigorous and severe than that in any boarding-school, that the kings of this century went into the Navy, where only rank matters and title and birth count for naught. There, if George V's experience is anything to go by, they discovered that their royal birth was, in fact, a distinct disadvantage. With true naval thoroughness, his superiors, George V revealed, went out of their way to take him down a peg; in fact, some took a particular delight in bullying and oppressing him whilst they could, because they knew that later they would not have the opportunity. Besides, it was a tale stored up for their grandchildren of the time that they set the King of England about some particularly menial task.

Constitutionally, of course, the decision with regard to the form that Prince Charles's education shall take, rests with the Queen and her ministers. Although the right of motherhood is acknowledged in provision for a Queen Consort to have the care of an heir to the throne during early childhood, the parental rights of the husband of a Queen Regnant are not admitted.

Undoubtedly, whatever the manner of Prince Charles's education, one factor that will not be overlooked will be the hope expressed by Mr. Churchill in the House of Commons at the time of the young prince's birth. "I hope," said Mr. Churchill, "that among those principles that will be instilled into him will be the truth that the sovereign is never so great as when the people are free. There we meet on common ground."

18

THE THREE GREAT RIGHTS

"THE Sovereign has, under a constitutional monarchy such as ours," wrote Walter Bagehot in his *English Constitution*, "three rights—the right to be consulted, the right to encourage, the right to warn."

Constitutionally, Queen Elizabeth cannot reject or oppose the advice of her ministers, but if she thinks the advice unsound she is entitled to express her opinion by warning them that it might be better not to follow the line of action proposed. The notion of professional statesmen, who have reached their position by long years of specialised experience and in the face of severe competition, consulting and being warned by a sovereign who owes his or her position entirely to accident of birth is not as ludicrous as it may seem. Governments change, ministers go out of power, but the sovereign remains permanently at the head of the nation, gaining an increasing practical experience on a wide and varied scale such as not even a prime minister enjoys. Quite obviously, no one can remain continually consulted and advised by the foremost brains in the country without gaining a wide experience and a wisdom and opinion of practical value to the interests of the nation. At present the direct influence of Queen Elizabeth springs primarily from her youth, from her youthful energy and enthusiasm which give an impetus to the profundity and prudence of her elder statesmen; but as the years pass and successive ministers appear on the scene, Queen Elizabeth will have the accumulated knowledge of how their predecessors and how the Opposition ministries tackled the problems of State. Those who fulfil her constitutional right of being consulted will be paying no mere lip-service to an abstract figurehead.

"A King, after a reign of ten years, ought to know much more of the working of the machine of Government than any other man in the country," declared Sir Robert Peel; while Benjamin Disraeli wrote to Queen Victoria: "For more than forty years your Majesty has been acquainted with the secret springs of every important event that has happened in the world and, during that time, has been in constant communication with all the most eminent men of your Kingdom. There must, necessarily, have accrued to a Sovereign, so placed, such a knowledge of affairs and of human character that the most gifted must profit by an intercourse with your Majesty, and the realm suffer by your Majesty's reserve."

The same advantage of youthful accession was shared by Queen Victoria and Elizabeth I who, with Queen Anne, have justifiably given birth to the belief that Britain always prospers with a woman on the throne. These were reigns of greatness indeed, but not one of those queens had greatness thrust upon her. It had to be earned.

The first Elizabeth ascended a throne perilously perched across a ravine, with the nation weak and impoverished and still cleft by religious discord. When Anne came to the throne she alone stood between the country and civil war. A series of Hanoverian kings, mostly lacking in character and abounding in debauchery, had brought the stock of monarchy very low when the Crown passed to Queen Victoria. Though the people turned with relief to the young Queen of eighteen, she quickly lost her initial popularity through her inexperience and im-

Central Press

Topical Press

Scenes from the State Opening of Parliament, November 1952

On the way to the Houses of Parliament

pulsiveness. The Lady Flora Hastings scandal, in which Victoria refused to take action against her court physician, who had wrongly diagnosed pregnancy and then gossiped about Lady Flora's condition, turned public sympathy against the young Queen. Graver still was her unconstitutional behaviour in showing political partisanship. When Sir Robert Peel was returned to power, Victoria refused to make any change in the appointments of her ladies of the bedchamber, and Peel thereupon declined to form a government. Triumphantly, Victoria called back Lord Melbourne to form a government, against the wishes of the electorate. As a result, the Queen's appearances in public were greeted with boos and catcalls of "Lady Melbourne." Possibly Peel took his stand as a matter of principle, but it says much for the influence of a young queen in times of a limited monarchy that a prime minister should fear the effect of having the wives and friends of the Opposition leaders in close association with her.

Personal monarchy died out with the first of the Georges who, being more interested in his German interests than in Britain, was content to leave the government entirely to parliament. In spite of an unsuccessful and unpopular attempt by George III to shake off the shackles of constitutional monarchy and rule, the principle that sovereigns reign but do not govern had become firmly established in the century before the Victorian era. Nevertheless, although the Crown's place in the Constitution had become virtually a symbol and figurehead, the success of the monarchy depended, as it still does, upon the person wearing the crown. When Queen Victoria shut herself up as a recluse for twenty-five years after the Prince Consort's death, the monarchy in Britain almost died. Never had the prestige of the Crown sunk lower, and in November

1871 a republican movement, backed in particular by Sir Charles Dilke and Joseph Chamberlain, and with John Bright as the potential first president of the Republic of the United Kingdom, began to catch hold in the country. There was partly a supporting influence from the spirit abroad in France, where the Third Republic had been established, but the main weapons of the movement were the arguments that the country was managing without a sovereign and was obtaining no return from the expenses of the throne, which were merely accumulating as the personal savings of the Queen.

The Times commented on the movement: "Englishmen know that Monarchy is an expensive institution, but they know also that a Republic, ostensibly cheaper, may really be dearer. Still more do they know that Revolution is the dearest alternative of all."

Before the republican movement could get properly under way, human interest saved the situation. The Prince of Wales fell ill with typhoid, and public sympathy switched at once to the royal family and particularly to his mother, the Queen, in her anxiety. After the Prince of Wales had recovered, attempts were made to restart the movement, but the three principals—Dilke, Chamberlain, and Bright—would have none of it.

The question of monarchy or republic came up once more in 1923, at the time that the Labour Party was emerging as a new political force. At their annual conference that year certain members tried to move the resolution, "That the Royal Family is no longer necessary as part of the British Constitution." The party leaders took exception to the motion, which was finally put to the conference as the question, "Is Republicanism the Policy of the Labour Party?" The answer was an overwhelming "No," supported by 3,694,000 votes against 386,000 would-be republicans.

Queen Victoria was a little, seventy-years-old lady in black when she finally succumbed to the persistent efforts of both Gladstone and Disraeli and emerged to restore the waning influence of her Crown. In her last ten years she proceeded to wipe from the memory her past mistakes and misfortunes and to set the throne securely on a base of solid respectability and achievement. She became the nation's grandmother, a martinet of a grandmother, perhaps, who none the less drew from the people a respect and desire to please and work for her.

There is no doubt that a woman on the throne brings out the innate chivalry in man and fires him with a more adventurous spirit, and to greater achievement. In the words of General Gordon: "England was made by adventurers, not by its Government, and I believe it will only hold its place by adventurers." It was thus with the first Elizabeth, inspiring men like Drake, Raleigh, Frobisher, and Hawkins to explore the unknown for the honour of the Queen. It is already so in the reign of the second Elizabeth, where men like the late John Derry and Neville Duke have heralded the scroll of achievement in the dimensions of space and sound.

The fact is apt to be overlooked that each age has had its discoveries and developments just as amazing to them as those of atomic energy and space exploration are to the present generation. Each age has ventured into an unknown fraught with the same sense of uncertainty, risk, and adventure. Throughout them all the Crown has remained steadfast, guided by those same basic principles that have applied equally to the national characteristics and way of life whether arrow, cannon-ball, or atom bomb has been the latest weapon, whether the Englishman's castle has been lit by rush-light or neon.

"God Save the Queen!" "Soldiers of the Queen." "Gentlemen, the Queen!" The words move and inspire as no other heartfelt prayer, proud catchphrase, or loyal toast could. They conjure up all the glories and traditions of the past, upon the foundation of which lies the promise of the future: a future built with the same boldness and vigour, the same steadfastness and stability. No government call to arms, no toast to any president or politician could provide the same stimulus and incentive, the same zealous, united response. Whether Conservative, Labour, Liberal, or Coalition, it is to the sovereign that the government turns in time of emergency to unite the country into a national fervour capable of yielding the final ounce of effort and endurance, and of mollifying personal tragedy and disaster. In a dictatorship, whatever the ideology, to disagree with the government is treason. A Briton can abominate his government and yet be an intensely loyal patriot.

Even within the small domestic realm of the United Kingdom the red tape of Whitehall administration comes in for frequent attacks by county councils and smaller local government authorities, closer in touch with local conditions and needs, as well as from the greater domains of Wales and Scotland, countries proud of their individual nationality. In Scotland the desire to shake off the yoke of Whitehall and manage its own affairs has found expression in the Scottish Covenant movement, amongst the leaders of which is the Countess of Erroll, Hereditary Lord High Constable and First Lady of Scotland after the Blood Royal. When it was suggested to her that self-government might be a stepping-stone to separation, she re-

plied at once: "Oh, no, the people of Scotland would never countenance that. The idea of complete separation is ridiculous. Why, the Crown is just as much Scottish as it is English."

Among the Dominions and other self-governing countries of the Commonwealth the feeling has ever been similar. The remoteness and officialdom of Whitehall have inspired no bond of loyalty or union, but as for the Queen—to the peoples of Australia and Canada the Crown is as much Australian or Canadian as it is English, Scottish, or British. The Queen is the Queen in Canada, the Queen in Australia, the Queen in every separate self-governing country within the Commonwealth, and it is in this sphere that she exercises her supreme influence, acting as herself, independent of Britain's Parliament. The fact that Britain has no monopoly of the Crown was made clear by the Statute of Westminster, 1931, which decreed that:

Inasmuch as the Crown is the symbol of the free association of the members of the British Commonwealth of Nations and as they are united by a common allegiance to the Crown, it would be in accord with the established constitutional position of all members of the Commonwealth in relation to one another that any alteration in law touching the succession to the Throne or the royal style and titles should hereafter require the assent of the Parliaments of all the Dominions as well as of the Parliament of the United Kingdom.

19

"VIVAT REGINA ELIZABETHA"

QUEEN ELIZABETH is the symbol of the national unity and continuity of each of the individual Commonwealth countries just as she is the embodiment of the wider integration of the Commonwealth as a whole. No matter how separate and different the policies and forms of government of the various nations, the Queen's position is no more affected than it is in the United Kingdom, where different governments follow their own distinct party doctrines. Throughout the Commonwealth her name, as Shakespeare said of Richard III, is "a tower of strength."

In 1937 Stanley Baldwin, in a farewell speech as Prime Minister, described the mystical union between this assortment of nations to a gathering of ten thousand young men and women from all parts of the Empire. The secret, he said, was "freedom, ordered freedom within the law, with force in the background and not in the foreground, a society in which authority and freedom are blended in proportion, in which the State and the citizens are both ends and means.

"It is an Empire," Mr. Baldwin continued, "organised for peace, and for the free development of the individual through an infinite variety of voluntary associations. It neither deifies the State nor its rulers. The old doctrine of the divine right of kings has gone, but we have no intention of erecting in its place a new doctrine of divine right of State.

"The young King and Queen whom we are delighted to

honour in these memorable days are the servants of the sovereign People. To them they have dedicated themselves. That is the magic of monarchy which is everlasting. The King is the symbol of the union, not only of an Empire, but of a society which is held together by the common view of the fundamental nature of man.

"If freedom of speech goes, then intolerance follows and justice is no more. The fruits of the free spirit of man do not grow in the garden of tyranny. As long as we have wisdom to keep the sovereign authority of this country as a sanctuary of liberty, a sacred temple consecrated to our common faith, men will turn from themselves towards us and draw their breath more freely."

The word Empire has fallen, officially, into disfavour. The "young King and Queen" have been replaced by an even younger Queen Regnant, their daughter; but the same spirit continues in the Commonwealth relationship. Were it not for the Queen, relations between each Commonwealth country would have to be defined by treaty and agreement. There is no written constitution for the Commonwealth any more than there is for the United Kingdom. Freedom is the keynote of the Commonwealth, freedom to belong to the brotherhood, freedom to owe allegiance to the Crown, freedom to separate and become an independent foreign country if one wishes. On being given self-government, Burma elected to leave the Commonwealth, and it was the United Kingdom that passed the Burma Independence Act, 1947, formally severing her relationship, just as in 1949 the Ireland Act satisfied Eire's desire to break off all ties. There is no compulsion on membership of the Commonwealth; no question of any enforced allegiance to the Crown. In fact, when India on gaining independence desired to remain within the Commonwealth and yet become a republic, provision was accordingly made.

The Declaration of London, issued after a meeting of the Commonwealth Prime Ministers in London in April 1949, stated:

"The Governments of the United Kingdom, Canada, Australia, New Zealand, South Africa, India, Pakistan, and Ceylon, whose countries are united as Members of the British Commonwealth of Nations and owe a common allegiance to the Crown, which is also the symbol of their free association, have considered the impending constitutional changes in India.

"The Government of India have informed the other Governments of the Commonwealth of the Intention of the Indian people that under the new constitution which is to be adopted India shall become a sovereign independent republic. The Government of India have, however, declared and affirmed India's desire to continue her full membership of the Commonwealth of Nations and her acceptance of the King as the symbol of free association of its independent member nations and as such the Head of the Commonwealth.

"The Governments of the other countries of the Commonwealth, the basis of whose membership of the Commonwealth is not hereby changed, accept and recognise India's continuing membership in accordance with the terms of the declaration.

"Accordingly the United Kingdom, Canada, Australia, New Zealand, South Africa, India, Pakistan, and Ceylon, hereby declare that they remain united as free and equal members of the Commonwealth of Nations, freely co-operating in the pursuit of peace, liberty, and progress."

In the case of India, allegiance to Queen Elizabeth is no longer the binding factor, but she still remains the essential link as the "symbol of the free association of its independent members and as such the Head of the Commonwealth."

With other member-nations, particularly those like Canada and Australia, which spring largely from British stock and look upon Britain as the "Old Country" or "Mother Country," there is no foundation for believing that anything other than allegiance to the Queen would hold them to the United Kingdom. After the Abdication Crisis in 1937 Mr. Lapointe, Canadian Minister of Justice, said categorically in the Federal Parliament of Canada:

"I desire to say today that the British Throne is the cement, the bond that unites all of us, and if it should disappear and be replaced by some other form, I am afraid that the end of the British Empire would be in sight and that Canada would soon not be part of the British Commonwealth of Nations."

It was Mr. Lapointe, then Canada's Minister of Marine, who in 1923 had first established a Dominion's right to act directly under the Crown and indpendent of any British minister. The occasion was a treaty between Canada and the United States for the purpose of protecting the halibut fisheries in the North Pacific. On the grounds that the matter affected Canada only and was no concern of the Imperial Parliament, Mr. Lapointe refused to allow the presence of the British ambassador to Washington at the discussions or his counter-signature on the treaty. By-passing the United Kingdom parliament completely, he obtained the assent of the Crown and signed with full plenipotentiary powers on behalf of King George V.

Already in the young Queen Elizabeth's reign Australia and New Zealand have demonstrated that it is to her alone that they are reponsible, by their refusal to invite representatives of the British Parliament to their discussions with the United

States on the question of defence measures in the Pacific.

In the unique relationship that Queen Elizabeth bears between the various independent members of the Commonwealth it is feasible that she may be offered different advice in different countries. Queen Elizabeth is powerless to act for the whole Commonwealth in unison. In a state of emergency, for instance, she could find herself proclaiming war in one part of the Commonwealth and a state of neutrality in another. In the last war, although the United Kingdom declared war against Germany on September 3rd, 1939, it was not until September 10th that on the advice of his Canadian ministers King George VI declared a state of war between Canada and Germany, whilst Eire, whose relationship to the Commonwealth was then one of external association, remained neutral for the duration.

At the time of the Italian-Abyssinian dispute it was only by thirty-three votes to twenty-two that the Australian House of Representatives agreed to follow the United Kingdom's lead and impose sanctions against Italy. Previously a motion for Australia's withdrawal from the League of Nations Union, supported by the argument that "the language of Downing Street was not that of Australia," had been defeated by six votes.

In domestic matters of trade or emigration, for example, in which two or more Commonwealth countries are concerned, it is not inconceivable that Queen Elizabeth might find herself offered conflicting advice by her respective ministers. Should such a situation arise there is no doubt that the Queen would then fulfil a vital role as mediator, using her personal influence to draw her conflicting ministers together and help them to find agreement. It is true that in 1910 when King George V wished to see the Opposition leaders about the Parliament Bill,

Mr. Asquith objected that, "It is not the function of a Constitutional Sovereign to act as arbiter or mediator between rival parties or policies." The King, however, insisted on the grounds that he was seeking not advice, which had already been tendered to him, but first-hand knowledge of the Opposition views, and Mr. Asquith gave way.

Although personal monarchy, in the sense of direct personal government by the sovereign, died with George I, in another sense the monarchy has become more personal than ever, both at home and throughout the Commonwealth. The Crown may be to all intents and purposes an idea, an ideal, that cloaks government, as Bagehot says, with the strength of religion, but it is the character of the sovereign which gives substance and reality to that idea.

Through press, photograph, radio, television, and films, Queen Elizabeth is better known as a person to her peoples than any other sovereign. Every important event of her life through childhood, her coming-of-age, her marriage, her motherhood, her accession, has been followed with proud interest and shared with a sense of family closeness and intimacy by her subjects.

Before her accession she was already well advanced on a programme that was bringing her personal acquaintance with the self-governing countries of the Commonwealth. Australia, New Zealand, and Ceylon are already preparing to welcome her in the near future, when she sets off once again on the tour from which she had to return so tragically in February 1952. Then only the peoples of Pakistan will remain to welcome their Sovereign on their own soil.

"Our ancient monarchy renders inestimable services to our country and to all the British Empire and Commonwealth of

Nations," declared Mr. Churchill in the House of Commons in November 1948. "Above the ebb and flow of party strife, the rise and fall of ministries and individuals, the change of public opinion or of public fortune, the British monarchy presides, ancient, calm and supreme within its functions, over all the treasures that have been saved from the past and all the glories we write in the annals of our country. . . ."

Those glories cannot be written, it is obvious, by Queen Elizabeth alone. "Kings cannot reign unless their subjects give," wrote Dryden; and, as Princess Elizabeth, the Queen made it clear that her twenty-first birthday vow of dedication to the service of ourselves and the "great imperial family to which we all belong" was possible only if the people themselves shared in it. Her throne must find its foundation in the hearts of subjects if the burden of monarchy is to be made bearable for her, and her functions as sovereign are to have a real and practical value. "As he is of the greatest power," wrote Bacon of the sovereign, "so he is subject to the greatest cares, made the servant of his people, or else he were without a calling at all. He then that honoureth him not is next an atheist wanting the fear of God in his heart."

If I may be pardoned the effrontery, I would like to adapt some lines that Tennyson wrote "To the Queen" to provide a particularly appropriate toast for Queen Elizabeth the Second —Elizabeth, Our Queen—and the future that lies before her.

> "Her court be pure; her life serene,
> God give her peace; her land repose;
> A thousand claims to reverence close
> In her as Mother, Wife and Queen."

So let it be.

ACKNOWLEDGMENTS

AMONGST a welter of authorities and references, I should like particularly to acknowledge the help I received, in preparing the outline of the Crown's part in the Constitution, from the following books:

A King's Story, H.R.H. the Duke of Windsor, K.G.; *Constitutional Law*, E. C. S. Wade and G. Godfrey Phillips; *The Law and Custom of the Constitution*, Sir William R. Anson; *Cabinet Government*, Sir W. Ivor Jennings; *This Realm of England*, Sir John Marriott; *The English King*, Michael Macdonagh; *The King and the Imperial Crown*, A. Berriedale Keith; *Crown, People and Parliament*, William Edwards; *Crown of England*, Erskine of Marr; *Constitutional History of England*, George Burton Adams; *Thoughts on the Constitution*, the Rt. Hon. L. S. Amery.